ILLUSTRATED HISTORY SERIES

To commemorate the 150th anniversary of the Great
Famine, Wolfhound Press commissioned a short, factual
history of this shattering event. The first volume of what
became an Illustrated History Series was written by Helen
Litton and published in 1994. Five more books followed *The
Irish Famine*:

- *The Irish Civil War*
- *The Celts*
- *Irish Rebellions 1798–1916*
- *Oliver Cromwell*
- *The World War II Years – The Irish Emergency*

This series of popular histories is designed to provide a
simple, clearly written introduction to a particular topic or
period for anyone interested in Irish history. *The Vikings* is
the seventh book in the Illustrated History Series and has
been written by Ailbhe MacShamhráin.

HELEN LITTON

2002

The Viking warrior of myth, the terror of the Northern seas on whom modern archaeology has cast the light of reality. Wash drawing (English, 1910).

The Vikings

AN ILLUSTRATED HISTORY

Ailbhe MacShamhráin

WOLFHOUND PRESS

Published in 2002 by

WOLFHOUND PRESS
an imprint of Merlin Publishing
16 Upper Pembroke Street
Dublin 2
Ireland

publishing@merlin.ie
www.merlin-publishing.com

ISBN 0-86327-848-5

British Library Cataloguing in Publication Data
A catalogue record for this book is available from the British Library.

Series Editor: Helen Litton
Cover Design: Slick Fish Design, Dublin
Cover Photograph: 8/9th century figure stone fragment, depicting a ship.
Height 175cm. Found at Tjaengvide, Alskog Ksp., Gotland, Sweden. AKG London.

Typesetting: Carrigboy Typesetting Services
Printed in Ireland by Colour Books Ltd., Dublin

PREFACE

This book, written mainly from an Irish perspective, aims to provide a general overview of Scandinavian and Irish relationships at the time of the Viking Expansion and after, and of the New World explorations that sprang from the Irish-Scandinavian milieu. It considers in turn the north-European homeland that generated Scandinavian culture, the Viking raids and the alliances that followed, the North Atlantic explorations and, finally, the Scandinavian heritage shared by Ireland and other European countries.

I am greatly indebted to all those who helped bring this work to fruition, from initial research through the various stages of writing, revision and preparation for publication. Full marks to the staff of Merlin Publishing for their patience! Various people assisted me in different ways – reading early drafts, refining my translation of texts, sourcing materials for me, or discussing points of archaeological or historical interpretation. Some merit particular mention; Marie Fingleton, Dr. Liam MacCóil, Peter Costello, Linzi Simpson (Margaret Gowen & Co. Ltd., Archaeological Consultants), Professor Emeritus J.J. O'Meara and Dr. Howard Clarke (University College Dublin). A special word of thanks to Dr. Seán Duffy (Head of Department of Medieval History, Trinity College Dublin) who, aside from writing the foreword, read the complete typescript and gave freely of his advice. There may be instances in which I failed to heed counsel offered; in such cases, the responsibility is mine.

Ailbhe MacShamhráin
2002

THE AUTHOR

Ailbhe MacShamhráin is a graduate of University College Dublin and holds his doctorate from Trinity College Dublin, where he subsequently taught. He now lectures on the Medieval Irish Studies Programme at the National University of Ireland, Maynooth, and has published widely on themes of early and medieval Irish history and settlement.

FOREWORD

A mong the former civilisations of the world few retain the same fascination as the Vikings. However they effected it, they succeeded in leaving an imprint in the popular imagination that shows no signs of abating. The mental image, as with all stereotypes, bears only a passing resemblance to the reality of the Vikings and their world. True, they were a warrior race, masters of the ocean waves in their elegantly and expertly crafted longships, and, at least to begin with, a pagan threat to much of the Christian infrastructure of maritime Europe and beyond. They were raiders, they were slavers, they could wreak destruction if they so chose, and frequently did, and they could certainly cause something not far short of hysteria to break out among the victims of their assaults. And yet we know that there is another side to the Vikings.

Their navigational skills led to the discovery of Iceland and Greenland, and they were in North America half a millennium or more before Columbus. They were, therefore, agents of European expansion, colonisers who did not simply destroy what they found and return home with their booty, but who left their Scandinavian homeland in search of, literally, greener pastures.

History has been far kinder to the Normans who conquered England in 1066, and yet they were the descendants of Vikings: the feudal system fostered by the Normans, and the chivalric knight that is the stereotypical image of the latter, is the creation of the Vikings who settled in what is now northern France. More important still is the fact that we must look to the Vikings for the origin of many of the most important towns and cities in north-western Europe, surely their greatest contribution to world civilisation. Almost everything that is characteristic of medieval life and thought, is the product of towns: it is towns that gave rise to civil autonomy, to the need to manage the citizens' common affairs, to the desire to protect and regulate their crafts and trade, and to the intellectual stimulation that was the origin of the university. The Vikings, therefore, contributed enormously to the making of Europe, and the world, as we know it today.

So, it is hugely important that our understanding of Viking civilisation becomes more sophisticated and less simplistic than the popular perception that has come down to us. Scholars – historians, archaeologists, art-historians, students of literature and others – have made enormous strides in recent decades in advancing our comprehension of the nature and dynamic of Viking life, but it has been slow to percolate into public awareness. Ailbhe MacShamhráin, one of the most gifted Irish medievalists of his generation, has produced in this delightful book both a synthesis of the most up-to-date scholarship on the Vikings and has given us many of his own insights, the product of many years' research, particularly on the impact of the Vikings on Ireland and its neighbours. It is a joy to read, it is a privilege to be associated with it, and it is a pleasure to recommend to anyone, raw recruit and weary veteran alike, with an interest in learning more about the Age of the Vikings.

Seán Duffy
Head of Dept. Medieval History
Trinity College Dublin
2002

Introduction

Vikings and other Scandinavians

Some, perhaps, thought of themselves as vikings; but the majority of Northmen who embarked on maritime expeditions, even if on occasion they resorted to the sword, probably saw themselves as adventurer-explorers if not as actual traders. The term 'viking' (from Old Norse *víkingr*), which means 'pirate' or 'sea-raider', gained widespread currency precisely because this less savoury aspect of Scandinavian seamanship made the deepest impression on contemporary Continental observers – most of whom were churchmen. The English cleric Alcuin, clearly shocked by the raid on Lindisfarne in 793, was only one of many commentators who expressed righteous anger at what they saw as the plunder and slaughter of Christendom by savage heathens.

The image of the murdering buccaneer was carried into modern scholarship and with it the term 'viking'. Therefore, as the disciplines of history and archaeology developed, it became acceptable to describe the culture of medieval Scandinavia as 'Viking Age'. Given the original meaning of 'viking', this is probably even less complimentary than describing the culture and society of nineteenth-century America as that of the 'Cowboy Age'. It is certainly ironic that present-day scholars, aside from discussing the history of viking raiding (where the term might be accurately applied), refer to 'viking society', the 'viking economy', or 'viking art and literature'. The survival of the term, as we enter the twenty-first century, can be justified only by the fact that it is a convenient shorthand.

However, it is probable that most natives of Europe's medieval northern fringe never left their home territory, whether across the sea or overland. While their maritime tradition was very strong, the majority, no doubt, had more experience of fishing boats than of viking longships. In terms of identity, they thought of themselves simply as Scandinavians, or as inhabitants of the particular region in which they were born and lived their lives. They were the people and theirs was

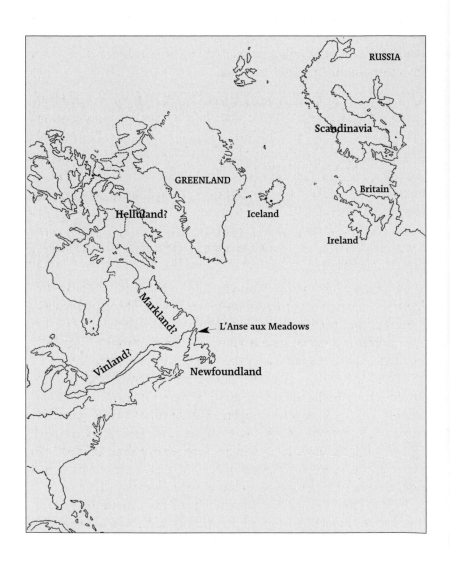

*Scandinavian homeland and overseas settlements. (Question marks for Helluland, Vinland and
Markland reflect uncertainty of scholarly opinion about locations.)*

the homeland which produced the viking raiders, but their everyday life, generally, was peaceful and domestic in character. More to the point, their cultural achievement was no less worthy of celebration than that of other medieval societies.

Iulius Solinus in his Collectanea says about Germany and its islands: In this region and in all the area of the north there are numerous bisons, which are like wild cattle, with shaggy necks and bristling manes. They can run faster than bulls; when captured, they cannot be tamed. . . .
There is also the elk which may be likened to the mule, whose upper lip hangs down so much that it can feed only by walking backwards . . . . Of the Germanic islands, Scandinavia is the greatest, but there is nothing great in it beyond itself.

Dicuil, *The Book on the Measurement of the Earth*, vii, paras 16–18.
Dicuil, a monk of Iona, was an Irish cleric and geographer who wrote in the 820s.

Classical writers such as Plinius Secundus (Pliny) and Julius Solinus knew of the existence of Scandinavia, but these and later geographers who drew upon their work, including the Irishman Dícuil who lived in the early ninth century, assumed it to be an island. Besides, they show no knowledge of its regions or the various peoples which inhabited them. As late as the eleventh century, the German cleric Adam of Bremen, although he could distinguish between Denmark, Sweden and Norway, still displayed a very imperfect knowledge of the physical and human geography of Scandinavia. He believed, for instance, that much of Denmark was barren salt desert and that the population of northern Norway, which included bearded women and men dressed in animal pelts, lived wild in the woods and subsisted on hunting alone.

Fortunately, we have the testimony of the late-ninth century merchant Óttarr who hailed, as it happens, from northern Norway. He visited the court of Alfred the Great, king of Wessex, where his description of his homeland and of his adventures was written down in Old English. Óttarr outlines the geography and political layout of Scandinavia as it was around the middle of what might be called the 'Viking Age'. According to his own account, he lived in Hålogaland –

the north-central region of Norðweg, or Norway. In the extreme north lived the Saami who, like the Cwénas further east along the Gulf of Bothnia, were a Finnish people. Immediately east and south of Norway was Sweoland, a territory which consisted of central and south-central Sweden. Further south was Denamearc (Denmark), whose kings ruled the peninsula of Jutland and its adjacent islands, Gotland in the eastern Baltic, the south of modern Sweden and the Oslofjord region of Norway.

> ... Northmannia is the farthest country of the world .... On account of the roughness of its mountains and the immoderate cold, Norway is the most unproductive of all countries, suited only for herds .... those who are removed beyond the Arctic tract along the ocean ... it is said, are to this day so superior in the magic arts or incantations that they profess to know what everyone is doing the world over ....
>
> I have heard that women grow beards in the extremely rough alps of that region, and that men live in the woods, rarely exposing themselves to sight. They use the pelts of wild beasts for their clothing and in speaking to one another are said to gnash their teeth rather than to utter words ....
>
> Adam of Bremen, *History of the Archbishops of Hamburg-Bremen*, 210, 211, 212. Adam, a German cleric, wrote his History around 1075 AD.

Clearly, in Óttarr's day, the various population groups of Scandinavia were assuming their own separate identities. The earlier situation is less clear. Archaeologists and prehistorians distinguish between an Early Iron Age (which saw the introduction of iron technology, and included the 'Migration Period'), which spanned the fifth and sixth centuries AD, and a Later Iron Age with two marked phases from *c.*550 to 800 and from *c.*800 to 1050, when the Iron Age finally gives way to the High Middle Ages. During the 'Migration Period', the peoples of Scandinavia spoke a common northern Germanic language, which is reflected in early inscriptions executed in the runic alphabet – often on standing stones known as runestones. In the sixth and seventh centuries, linguistic changes led to a distinctively Scandinavian speech. Later still, a divide along east-west lines meant that Danish/Swedish and Norwegian/Icelandic formed two language sub-groups within the Scandinavian world.

> Othere told his lord, King Alfred, that he lived the furthest north of all the Norwegians. He said that he lived in the north of Norway on the coast of the Atlantic. He also said that the land extends very far north beyond that point, but it is all uninhabited, except for a few places here and there where the Finnas have their camps, hunting in winter and in summer fishing in the sea.
>
> Othere (Ottarr), *Description of Norway*, 18.
> Ottar, a Norwegian aristocrat, merchant and farmer, who flourished in the 890s, visited the court of the English king, Alfred.

The closing years of the eighth century saw large-scale expansion into insular and Continental Europe. Undoubtedly, this movement had a significant 'viking' dimension and these elements, whether bands of privateers or 'official' expeditionary forces, attracted more than their fair share of notice. But following these raiders came settlers from the fjords and coastal plains of Scandinavia – fisher-farmers, craftsmen and traders. They pressed eastwards into Russia, while others moved westwards establishing colonies in parts of Britain and Ireland, and in Normandy. Later, a movement further west – across the north Atlantic to the 'New World' – involved both Norwegian and Irish participation. This short book, written primarily from an Irish perspective, aims to explore this period and its aftermath.

1. PEOPLE OF THE NORTHERN LANDS

Travellers, Traders and Farmers

By the Early Iron Age (400–550 AD), the strong maritime tradition of Scandinavia was already well developed. The sea was important not only for fishing but for trade and social connections, given that Denmark included quite a number of islands and that Norway, in particular, had such a long fragmented coastline. Not surprisingly, there was a tendency for settlements to follow main sailing routes. In Norway, archaeologists have discovered several early occupation sites on islands such as Leknes and Bjarkøy. Further south and east, in Denmark and Sweden, centres for maritime trade grew up close to rich settlement sites known to have been political centres in pre-Viking times. Sea connections helped the development of trading colonies in Estonia and Latvia even before 700 AD.

Overland travel was presumably undertaken by Scandinavians from earliest times – whether by horse or foot. Harsh winter conditions and heavy snowfalls posed a challenge, but sledges of ninth-century date have been found at Oseberg and elsewhere, while skiing is mentioned in Skaldic poetry. Nonetheless, evidence for purpose-built facilities for overland travel is not plentiful outside of Denmark and southern Sweden, and tends to be of relatively late date. The oldest known bridge in Scandinavia, that over the River Vejle near Jelling in Jutland, has been dated by radio-carbon tests to 979 (+/–1 year). Several fords and causeways are known from the tenth century or later, while a number of Swedish rune-stones from the twelfth century commemorate local gentry who engaged in the building or clearance of roads.

The economy of Scandinavia was already quite developed by the time the period of viking raids commenced in the late eighth century. In general, the agricultural potential of Denmark and of southern Sweden was greater than that of Norway. Scandinavian cultivation methods involved intensive fertilization, mixing animal manure with peat and humus, so that the soil did not have to lie fallow for periods of time, as was common practice in Continental Europe. Already by

Early Christian stone, Jelling, Jutland, featuring representation of Christ.

The Norwegian Oseberg ship, during the course of excavation, 1904.

the eighth century, they were producing high yields of barley, oats and rye. Many houses had tillage plots, where they grew cabbage, peas and beans. Livestock farming was certainly not overlooked: cattle were important to the economy and sheep and goats were also raised. Domestic poultry were kept and, while there is no evidence that bees were domesticated, southern Scandinavians were certainly familiar with honey as a sweetener: they may have collected wild honey. It seems that they also collected wild hops, for use in brewing. Their food supply was certainly augmented by gathering, quite apart from hunting and, of course, fishing.

In Norway, geographical factors posed more of a challenge to agriculture, with intensive cultivation possible only in the south. Here, however, there are indications that the area under tillage increased from c.600 AD. From about this time, quite extensive woodland clearance was taking place at Borre in the Vestfold region. New herbs were introduced and, as fertilization methods were more widely adopted, yields of barley and oats increased. The fact that these developments parallel the transition to the later Iron Age may be significant. The characteristic burial mounds of this period seem to suggest a new social organisation; the emergence of a new political elite could certainly explain both this apparent social restructuring and the extension of agriculture in the south.

They browse their cattle, like the Arabs, far off in the solitudes. In this way do the people make a living from their livestock, by using the milk of the flocks or herds for food and the wool for clothing . . . .

In many places in Norway and Sweden cattle herdsmen are even men of the highest station, living in the manner of patriarchs and by the work of their own hands.

Adam of Bremen, *History of the Archbishops of Hamburg-Bremen*, 211, 212.

Further north, livestock farming predominated. Many parts of Norway had limited agricultural potential; extensive mountain ranges, forests and swamps restricted the availability of farmable land. Yet even some of the less hospitable areas apparently experienced a degree of agricultural expansion during the 'Viking Age'. Certain placenames with elements indicating agriculture point to a tenth-century or earlier date. The element *staðr* (a stead, farm), commonly found in eastern Norway and in the Trøndelag region, must be early in order to have been imported into the Scottish islands, the Faroes and Iceland. *Staðr* most often means a dairy farm, but the element *garðr* points to tillage. Specifically, it describes an enclosed tillage area, often with a farm-house and outbuildings. These tillage enclosures often had adjacent grazing land. However, most holdings – especially in central to northern Norway – seem to have been modest enough, with their owners engaging in mixed farming. This was so even for the local nobility. The above-mentioned Óttarr of Hålogaland, who visited England at the end of the ninth century, is a case in point. Although he described himself

He was among the chief men in that country, but he had not more than twenty cattle, twenty sheep and twenty pigs, and the little that he ploughed he ploughed with horses ....

He said that the land of the Norwegians is very long and narrow. All of it that can be used for grazing and ploughing lies along the coast and even that is in some places very rocky.

Othere (Ottarr), *Description of Norway*, 20.

as 'one of the leading men of his territory', his farm was stocked with just twenty cows, twenty sheep and twenty pigs, and he had only one arable field. Óttarr was clearly a man of means, but not as a result of farming. As a nobleman, he collected tributes – particularly from the Saami of the far north. He also fished and hunted; he tells us that he pursued whales and walrus. By exploiting the region's natural resources in this way, he was able to increase his wealth through trade. Men of lesser status no doubt also hunted to supplement the meagre living they could make from the land.

Industry and Craftwork

The economy of the 'viking homeland' was not, however, dependent solely on agriculture. Many of the industries and crafts for which the Scandinavian diaspora would later become famous were well established long before the time of the vikings. One could perhaps class as 'heavy industry' the extraction of minerals, iron production and shipbuilding. While the technology for mining iron ore may not have been available, deposits of bog iron were exploited at a number of locations – in some instances from as early as the first century or at least by the sixth. Areas in which iron extraction was carried on included Norrland and Småland in Sweden, around Dokkfløy in southern Norway, around Lake Møs in Telemark and in the Trøndelag region. The production of iron was improved from as early as the seventh century by the development of permanent shaft ovens. This meant that slag could be collected at the side instead of filling the oven bottom and

Rune stone from circa 1000 AD, Nationalmuseet, Copenhagen.

so rendering it unusable for further processing of ore. It became common for smelting sites in Scandinavia to be roofed over and, on occasion, buildings were purposely constructed to house smelters. Iron production grew from c.900 onwards, while the mining of copper in the Dalarna area of Sweden may have commenced in the tenth or eleventh centuries. Steatite was also widely extracted. This 'soapstone', soft enough to be cut with a knife, was used for the manufacture of a range of utensils. Pieces of steatite were also employed as whetstones, while lava was quarried to make quernstones for grinding corn.

Shipbuilding was conducted on a commercial scale, long before the time of the vikings, at several Scandinavian ports – notably at Hedeby in Denmark. It is commonly assumed that pre-viking ships were solely dependent on rowers – rather small, slow vessels compared with the later 'longships' which made effective use of sails. Certainly, the seventh-century 'Kvalsund ship' is a rowing vessel, but picture stones from Gotland, which date to roughly the same time, depict sailing craft. By the eighth century, however, Scandinavian ship-wrights had made significant advances in technology, and a new style of vessel appeared. These were symmetrical and clinker-built – which means that the timbers from which they were constructed overlapped slightly instead of being abutted. The addition of a keel meant that these craft were less likely to capsize. Examples from Oseberg and Gokstad in Norway resemble typical warships of the ninth or tenth centuries, although the elaborately decorated Oseberg craft was probably purely ceremonial. Merchant vessels of the period are represented by that from Åskekarr in Sweden and two (of five ships found) from Skuldelev in Denmark.

An extensive range of craftwork was carried out especially at such large centres as Hedeby, or Birka in Sweden. Iron was used for a range of weapons and tools, locks, chains and horse trappings. Other metals worked included bronze, while jewellery was manufactured occasionally in gold but most commonly in silver. Brooches and pins, necklaces, pendants and arm-rings have all been found in large quantities. Various wood-crafts were also practised; carpentry for building and for house-

Norse men and women in tenth-century costume. Modern drawing from The
Saga of Olaf Tryggvason *(London, 1911)*

hold items, coopering and turning for making vessels and ornamental
items, and basket-making. In addition, textiles were produced from
wool, linen, imported silk and wild furs; they even fashioned imitation
furs from cloth. Scandinavia also had its leather and bone industries,
making footwear and bags, combs and other accessories.

Some of the portable craft products, especially items of jewellery,
leather and bone, were exported. As wealth increased from the
proceeds of viking raids, the scope of foreign trade expanded. Exports
of Scandinavian raw materials and manufactured goods could be
supplemented with the proceeds of plunder and slaving, to pay for
importing such luxury goods as silk and spices, wines, pottery and
glassware. The growth of commerce prompted the development of
systems of weights and of coinage. As early as *c.*800, coins were being
minted in Hedeby. By the end of the first millennium, Swedish and
Norwegian kings were issuing their own coins.

House and Home

As might be expected, the level of economic development from one Scandinavian region to another greatly influenced the pattern of settlement. In Denmark, where agriculture was most intense and commerce most advanced, the overall trend was towards clustered settlement. Typically, outside of main centres, people lived in small villages or hamlets like Vorbasse in Jutland. Relocated and rebuilt several times over the centuries, as the surrounding land became exhausted, Vorbasse in the eighth century consisted of seven farm houses, each with fenced-in plots, on either side of a little streetway. Further north and west, however, settlement became increasingly dispersed. In Norway, isolated farmsteads were the norm.

The houses themselves showed local variation in design and in construction. As a general rule, timber houses, whether post-and-wattle or stave built, gave way to earthen and even turf dwellings in northern regions, where timber was scarce. Matters of design and layout also changed over time. Up to the eighth century, the most common house-type was the Iron Age 'long house', with a byre built on to the living quarters. There is a fine example at Borg in Lofoten, Norway. Originally, this building was 55m in length, but in the late seventh or early eighth century it was enlarged to an impressive 83m. By the end of the same century, however, house styles were apparently becoming more diversified. The 'Viking hall' (such as that at Oma in Jæren), which many consider typical, is gradually supplanted by a small rectangular house-type.

Picture-stone from Hammars, Gotland, Sweden

The notion of a large all-purpose building is gradually replaced by a group of smaller buildings with different functions, so that a separate byre and outbuildings become common. At Jarlshof in Shetland, a modest rectangular farmhouse stood within a complex of buildings which included a barn or byre, a stable and a smithy. As this trend was imported into 'Viking Age' settlements abroad – including Ireland – it is probable that such house-types existed in Scandinavia (and in Norway in particular) before 800. Houses tended to reflect the status of their owners – not only in size but in fittings. The homes of the more prosperous were commonly decorated with wood-carvings and with paint, the interior walls hung with tapestries and the floors strewn with rugs. Furnishings typically included chairs, stools and wooden chests, while beds could be lined with feather and down.

The occupants of these houses had a short life-expectancy by present-day standards. On the evidence of burials, relatively few people lived into their forties and even fewer exceeded the age of 55. Physical remains commonly show clear signs of osteo-arthritis. The daily routine of life was hard, whether on the farm or at sea, and disease was rife. Combs and other 'toilet implements', commonly found at settlement sites, suggest that early Scandinavians were concerned with grooming themselves but, like other medieval peoples, understood little about hygiene in the broader sense. As to appearance several Gotland picture-stones illustrate conventions of dress, while finds of textile fragments and accessories help to fill out the picture. Silver figures found at various locations in Sweden represent elegant women with graceful posture. They are dressed in long trailing gowns, decoratively embroidered; some have mantles over their shoulders held in place by brooches. They wear their hair long, tied in a stylish knot on top or at the back of their heads. In some cases, their outfit is completed with a hair-net or veil. Presumably such finery was worn only by ladies of high status and even then, perhaps, only for special occasions.

Everyday clothing for women consisted of ankle-length dresses, often pleated, over which they wore a pinafore-like garment. This was held up by shoulder-straps and, typically, fastened above breast level by a pair of tortoise-shell-shaped brooches made of bronze. Men are represented in trousers displaying a range of styles, from calf-length to full-length, straight and flared. Above this, they wore belted tunics and, usually, a short cloak fastened at the shoulder with a brooch. The materials at their disposal included wool and linen – with furs and even silk providing further options for the higher classes. Various natural dyes were available, and even two-toned garments are attested, as well as appliqué decoration and items made of one material trimmed with another. However, stylish clothing was in all probability confined to the privileged; the bulk of the population probably wore plain garments of undyed wool.

Society

Medieval Scandinavian society, as reflected in the provincial laws such as the *Frostuping*, was markedly stratified and aristocracy-dominated. The magnates, who probably held the larger farms for which archaeological evidence is available, occupied the higher levels of a social pyramid. Beneath them were the free classes, which included professional warriors, learned grades, farmers, merchants and certain craftsmen. There may well have been freeholders, although the evidence is slight; it seems clear, however, that the majority of farmers were tenants dependent on the higher orders. At the bottom of the social scale were the *thralls*, in effect a class of slaves. Slavery was an institution in pre-viking times; even tenant farmers kept unfree workers. Of course, it did not follow that all slaves were badly treated. Some of the more comely female slaves, because they could please their masters sexually, won favour on that count. There may have been loyal household slaves who earned the affection of their owner's family – while others would have been valued because of skill in craftwork. The value accorded to certain categories of slave made possible a degree of social mobility; some were rewarded with grants of freedom, and set themselves up as small tenant-farmers or as craftsmen.

Nineteenth-century historians speculated that property was held in common in this society. Because it seemed from the study of other

Germanic cultures that land was owned by the extended family, it was argued that the eleventh-century Scandinavian Provincial Laws reflected a kin-based society. However, close examination of the Provincial Laws shows that inheritance of property was through both male and female lines, which does not fit with a tightly kin-based society. On the contrary, it seems clear that the nuclear family consisting of parents and children was of prime importance. However, there are indications from archaeology and placename study that extended families sometimes lived in the same vicinity and so quite likely supported each other, whether in day-to-day living or in times of crisis. The extended family may not, therefore, have been the dominant factor in social organisation, but it certainly had an important role to play in social, legal and religious affairs.

Religion: Old and New

The question of religion, as understood and practised by Iron Age Scandinavians, poses many difficulties because of the scarcity of contemporary written sources. Archaeology can throw considerable light on ritual practices, but tells us little about what people believed in relation to their gods, or sought to achieve by religious rites. The names of certain deities are preserved in runic inscriptions, and representations of some can be recognised. There are some contemporary descriptions of rituals, such as that from the tenth-century Arab traveler Ibn Fadhlan, and Continental ethnographers – notably the late eleventh century Adam of Bremen – tried to summarise what they knew of the Scandinavian pantheon. There are elements of mythology reflected in a genre of Norse poetry known as Eddaic verse. Some examples of this, even if written down much later, may date back to the Viking Age. Finally, mythological episodes formed the basis for a genre of epic tales in the later medieval period – as was the case in Ireland. Overall, however, it is difficult to obtain an integrated picture of practice and belief, or to be certain that a god represented in a certain light by later medieval saga writers was viewed in the same way by people of the 'Viking Age' or earlier.

Surely the most dramatic ritual for which evidence survives is the ship burial. Ibn Fadhlan witnessed such a ceremony on the banks of the Volga River. The deceased chieftain was laid out in a ship with his weapons and all his finery, and a number of animals were purposely slain and placed with him, as well as a female slave who was subjected to repeated acts of ritual intercourse before being put to death. The ship was then solemnly burned with all its contents. The remains of several ship burials have been found although not all were all as elaborate as that described. Two from the vicinity of Avalsnes, in Norway's Rogaland province, are thought to be eighth century. That from Borre in Vestfold is later, and probably dates to about 900 AD. However, the vast majority of burials, including those in the cemeteries around Avalsnes and Borre, were deposited in plain barrows, or mounds. Cremation was not the only rite practised; interment is widely attested. Members of the aristocracy have been found buried with a range of accoutrements for use in the next life, including food and drink vessels, weapons, tools, gaming pieces and, not uncommonly, horses or dogs – perhaps favourite pets. On occasion, as in a burial at Stengade on the Danish island of Langeland, a slave followed his master to the grave. Here, a freeman (he was apparently dressed in a linen garment and carried a spear) is accompanied by another male who was decapitated and whose feet appear to have been bound together. But the burials found by archaeologists tend to be those of aristocrats, for whom impressive mounds were raised. Graves of ordinary folk – simple holes in the ground – are less likely to be discovered.

We have a limited understanding of the next world for which these deceased aristocrats, accompanied by their personal possessions, animals and slaves, were clearly destined. Valhalla, to which prominent warriors were led by the Valkyries (semi-divine female functionaries of the gods), was the realm of the heroic dead. The otherworld envisaged for women, or indeed for men of lesser standing, is not similarly honoured in saga. But Iron Age Scandinavians did believe in a parallel dimension peopled by gods and goddesses, the more prominent of whom are described by Adam of Bremen. Pre-eminent among the

Viking funeral, burning the warrior's body in his boat.
Wood engraving after a drawing by Alexander Zick (1845–1907).

gods was Odin, the ruler of Valhalla. Because of his exhalted position, he is neither represented by figures nor directly named in inscriptions – instead he is referred to by various aliases such as Gaut, or Ygg. In these guises he was associated with the arts, especially with poetry. It was believed that Odin was the father of Thor, the god who controlled the skies and the weather and who was invoked as a defender against evil. There is a depiction of Thor, wielding the hammer with which he is usually associated, on the Altuna stone from the Swedish province of Uppland. Pendants and brooches in the form of Thor's hammer are known from all over the 'Viking World'.

Another important deity was Frey, who features on plaques or is occasionally represented by a small bronze figure. He controlled fertility, whether in relation to humans, animals or crops, and is generally depicted with an over-large penis – or locked in embrace with his female counterpart, Freya. This Freya, aside from her own role in relation to fertility, commanded a cohort of warriors and presided over a hall in the realm of the dead. She was one of the most widely worshipped goddesses; another was Hel, queen of a shadowy underworld. Evidence for the spread of cults relating to these deities is provided by place-names. Odin is commemorated by the fjord, river and town of Odense on the island of Fyn, Denmark – and in the name of Odensbacken near the lake of Hjälmaren, in southern Sweden. Thor gives his name to Thorsø in Jutland, to Tórshavn in the Faroes and to Thórshöfn in northern Iceland. The name of the island of Frøja, off Trøndelag in Norway, bears testimony to a local cult of Frey.

> I am called a poet
> a true ship-wright of tall Vidhur
> discoverer and distributor of the gift of Gaut
> a true learned man of generosity
> the ale-provider of Ygg's company
> creative worker of the lays
> keen crafty smith of the metrical word
> what else is a poet truly?
>
> Eddaic verse; the reply of Bragi to the hag. (Translated by the author.)

However, by the time Adam of Bremen was compiling his ethnography in the late eleventh century, Scandinavia was already largely Christian. Some individual Danish rulers are known to have been baptised as early as the ninth century. Whether these early acceptances of Christianity were necessarily motivated by religious zeal – or by anticipation of political or commercial advantage – is beside the point. In the century that followed, Christianity made slow but steady progress northwards through Denmark. Around the same time, many Scandinavian colonists abroad, including those who had settled in Britain and Ireland, also accepted this new faith. Early in the eleventh century, Christianity took firm root in Sweden and Norway under kings Óláfr Tryggvason and Óláfr Haraldsson. The latter, who reigned from 1015 until he was overthrown in 1028, was the first to introduce a formal church organisation to Norway. He was later venerated as St. Olave. By the mid-eleventh century, Christianity was well established in the Scandinavian homeland, and had already spread to the fringe colonies, including Iceland.

Movement out of Scandinavia

It seems that the petty kingdoms of Denmark were well developed by the seventh to early eighth centuries, based around commercial and cult centres such as Hedeby or Odense. There are strong indications that Jutland, at least, had been brought under a centralised authority by the later eighth century. Danish kings had, by the ninth century, secured control of the surrounding islands and gradually extended their authority into the Vestfold area of Norway and the south of Sweden. Further north, the process of political unification was more protracted. Amongst the Norwegians, Haraldr *hárfagri* (the fine-haired), who flourished in the late ninth/early tenth century, was celebrated in skaldic poetry and in saga (composed two hundred years or more after his time) as the first king of all Norway.

The reality is probably more complex. Haraldr's mother was the daughter of a petty king of Sogn in west-central Norway; his own original realm, while not easy to identify, seems to have lain north and east of that province. His great victory at Hafrsfjord left him in control of Rogaland, and enabled him to build a more extensive overlordship, but it is unlikely that Haraldr exercised effective control beyond south-western Norway. By the same token Ólafr Skötkonung (d. 1020), who earned a prominent place in Swedish tradition, was the first to unite the kingships of the Svear and the Götar – but he was a long way from being king of all Sweden. Political unification then, at least as far as northern Scandinavia was concerned, was an eleventh-century development.

The timescale of such changes is clearly of vital importance in seeking to explain the phenomenon of the 'Viking Age'. It has been argued that extension of royal authority was a factor which drove regional nobles to embark on overseas adventure. However, this can hardly account for the initial phases of viking activity. Of course debate has persisted within certain historical and archaeological circles on dating the beginning of the 'Viking Age'; should it be dated from the earliest known record of raids at the end of the eighth century, or from a recognisable change in the archaeological record some time before? Certain weapon types and art motifs (including the 'gripping beast' motif and Berdal-type oval brooches), accepted as characteristic of the 'Viking Age', had appeared earlier in the eighth century. Ultimately, a degree of consensus emerged by the 1980s – that the historical record of raiding from *c.*790 AD should be taken as the principal marker. In any case, viking activity was under way before the end of the eighth century, and there is little to suggest that political unification had progressed very far by this time – least of all in Norway and Sweden. Furthermore, indications are that Danish control in these territories was limited to the southern reaches. Political pressure on the nobles may have been a factor in later phases of viking activity, but can hardly explain the initial 'tidal wave' which swamped so much of Europe.

Other possible causal factors behind the viking expansion include population growth which, some have argued, is traceable throughout the later Iron Age and is reflected in an extension of agricultural settlement. Many have seen the spread of placenames which include the elements *staðr* and *landr* as indicative of new settlement in Viking times; in this scenario, people moved from the coast up fjords and river valleys, putting pressure on an already settled population. Recent studies, however, have shown that this is not the full picture. Firstly, placenames of the *staðr/landr* class can predate the 'Viking period'. Furthermore, there are signs that population growth was not sustained throughout the Iron Age, at least not universally across Scandinavia. Circumstances may have created congestion in certain areas, notably in western Norway (an area from which some early viking raids appear to have been launched), but arguments that overpopulation explains the entire 'Viking phenomenon' are difficult to sustain.

In recent years, several scholars have tried to place settlement and viking activity alike in a commercial context. There are indications of contact of a non-hostile kind, whether it should be interpreted as settlement or simply as trade, across the North Sea before the end of the eighth century. There are hints of a Scandinavian presence in the Faroes and the use of reindeer antler for comb-making in Shetland and Orkney at an apparently early date; similarly, a few metal objects of British or Irish origin have been found in Norwegian graves which seem to pre-date the period of Viking raids. If Norwegian petty kings were in fact building a network of trade and of political alliances in northern Britain by the late eighth century, the commencement of the period of viking raids deserves to be viewed against this background.

The earliest record we have of a 'viking incident' concerns an affair on the coast of Dorset in 787. A reeve of King Beorhtric of Wessex was slain by men from *Heredaland*, perhaps Hordaland in Norway. Unfortunately, we have only the English version of the events that preceded the killing, but the fact that the man slain on this occasion was a reeve – a royal official – is almost certainly significant. Also worthy of note is the fact that Danish commercial interests were, if anything, even more developed by this time. Perhaps, as has recently been suggested by Scandinavian scholars, early Danish viking raids represented a response to a threat (real or perceived) to their trading interests in the North Sea. In this view, the 'viking phenomenon' was, at least in part, a commercially motivated conflict which gathered pace as Christian powers reasserted themselves against a 'pagan threat', and as Scandinavian political organization continued to develop.

AD 787. In this year King Beorhtric took Eadburh, King Offa's daughter to wife. And in his days first came three ships of Northmen from Haeretha land. And then the reeve rode thereto, and would drive them to the king's vill, for he knew not what they were, and they there slew him. Those were the first ships of Danish (sic) men that sought the land of the English race.

Benjamin Thorpe (ed.), *The Anglo-Saxon Chronicle*. London, 1861, ii, 47–8.

Timeline: People of the Northern Lands		
	Developments in Scandinavia	Developments elsewhere
400 Early Iron Age		
	The 'Migration Period'	
500		
Later Iron Age		
600		
	Expansion of tillage in Scandinavia	
	Improved iron production	
700		Scandinavian colonies in Estonia and Latvia
	Avalsnes ship-burial	
	Advances in shipbuilding	
800	New house types	Earliest Viking Expansion
	Coins minted at Hedeby	
		Settlement (mostly Norwegian and Danish) in Western Europe
		—
		Settlement (mostly Swedish) in the Baltic and in Russia
900	Haraldr hárfagri unites southern Norway	
	Borre Ship-burial	
	Christianity established in Denmark	
1000	Christianity reaches Sweden and Norway	
	Ólafr Skötkonung unites the Svear and Götar	
High Middle Ages		Adam of Bremen compiles his Ethnography

2. THE 'FURY OF THE NORTHMEN'

Adventurers or 'Pagan Pirates'?

From the perspective of observers, viking outside activity, commencing from the end of the eighth century, was sudden, violent, unprovoked and inexplicable except in terms of pagan fury against Christendom. Contemporary witnesses in Britain, Ireland and Continental Europe feared and resented viking aggression, regardless of the motives which may have prompted it. Commercial rivalry as a likely motivator for viking activity has already been discussed; this was a time of economic growth for Europe as a whole, and trading ports were thriving. It was also a time of political change, as petty kingdoms of the Early Christian period, often loosely structured, were giving way to larger territorially-based realms. Even in Ireland, which did not share the Continent's urban heritage, larger ecclesiastical centres were taking on some urban functions while powerful dynasties, like the Uí Néill in the north and midlands or the Uí Dúnlainge in Leinster, were forging the political shape of the island's 'Classical Age'.

For Scandinavian adventurers willing to take the risk, there was ample wealth available and a golden opportunity to exploit competing political forces in order to maximise their share. No doubt they knew, or soon realised, that their shipbuilding and seamanship gave them a clear advantage over most potential rivals in Europe. Whether they engaged in legitimate trade, settled to farm, extorted taxes, plundered valuables or launched violent attacks seemingly depended on the circumstances. Viking leaders need not always have shared a common outlook or level of ambition; besides, each location presented its own challenge. Available wealth could take different forms; in one case it could be merchandise, in another, natural resources. The adoption of peaceful or hostile strategies in any given situation may have depended on the defence of the intended target, on logistical difficulties, or simply on the readiness of the locals to yield or resist.

2cm

Detail of head of thistle brooch
(no location), see colour plate IV.

The Dorsetshire incident of 787, apparently involving a Norwegian ship's crew, may have been the result of a conflict of trading interests. Nevertheless, difficulties quickly escalated and within five years we find King Offa organising the defence of Kent against a Scandinavian threat. It is easier to ascribe politico-economic motives to the Danish attacks on the Carolingian Empire a few years later. The attacks on Frisia in 810, and the French coast in 820, were preceded by years of friction between the Empire and Denmark's King Godred, as Franks and Danes alike competed for control of the Elbe waterway. However, the sack of Lindisfarne off England's Northumbrian coast in 793, of Donemuthan monastery (location uncertain, but in the same region) in 794, and that of St. Philipert at the mouth of the Loire in 799, did involve violent attacks on ecclesiastical centres.

The viking attacks on churches attracted most attention from commentators – many of whom, as already remarked, were ecclesiastics. Alcuin of York condemned the plundering of Lindisfarne in no uncertain terms; he graphically related to King Aethelred of Northumbria how the Church of St. Cuthbert was left 'spattered with the blood of the

Lo, it is nearly 350 years that we and our fathers have inhabited this most lovely land, and never before has such terror appeared in Britain as we have now suffered from a pagan race, nor was it thought that such an inroad from the sea could be made. Behold, the church of St. Cuthbert spattered with the blood of the priests of God, despoiled of all its ornaments; a place more venerable than all in Britain is given as a prey to pagan peoples. ... Foxes pillage the chosen vine, the heritage of the Lord has been given to a people not his own; and where there was the praise of God, are now the games of the gentiles ....

Alcuin of York writing to King Aethelred of Northumbria, 793 AD.

Finds of tortoiseshell-shaped brooches like this indicate the presence of women amongst the earliest Scandinavian settlers in Ireland.

NATIONAL MUSEUM OF IRELAND

priests of God'. It is possible that an ideological point was being made here: that such 'pirates' deserved to be punished for their pagan character as much as for their violent assault. When the coasts of western Scotland and Ireland experienced viking raids from 795 onwards, Irish clergy added their voices to the already mounting cry raised against these attackers. One Irish chronicler, writing in 820, complains bitterly that there wasn't a harbour anywhere on the island's coast without vikings – certainly a gross exaggeration. Yet, a contemporary scribe, writing in Ireland, penned a verse in the margin of a work by the Roman grammarian Priscian; he was thankful for a spell of stormy weather, which would save his community from the threat of seaborne strikes.

The actual level of violence produced by early viking raids is difficult to gauge. Between 800 and 820 there are only seven years for which viking activity is recorded in the annals – scarcely endorsing the popular picture of an island swamped in mayhem. In the initial stages at least, many raiding parties consisted of only one to two hundred

Sharp is the wind tonight
it tosses the white mane of the sea
I do not fear (on such a night) the coursing of the great sea
by fierce warriors from the northern lands.

Anonymous scribe in a copy of *Priscian's Latin Grammar*, St. Gallen, Switzerland, mid ninth century. (Translation by the author.)

Viking footwear, a relic of everyday life, from the High Street, Dublin, Viking dig.

men. In 812, a viking force was slaughtered by the king of Umall, ruler of a petty territory on Ireland's west coast, who could hardly have mustered more than a few hundred soldiers. Nor were the vikings the only ones to plunder ecclesiastical sites in Ireland. Throughout much of the eighth century, as the record shows, religious foundations had been involved in so-called 'monastic battles'. Seemingly, churches and church properties were treated as 'legitimate targets' in warfare. For example, in 815, Cluain Crema (near Elphin, Co. Roscommon) was devastated and asylum-seekers killed within its sanctuary lands by the men of Bréifne (a border-kingdom between Connacht and Ulster). In 833, Clonmacnois was sacked by the king of Cashel, Fedelmid mac Crimthainn, himself a bishop. Yet the strongest condemnation was reserved for the vikings. Perhaps their style of warfare was viewed as more 'total', or else the pagan character of these raiders (the Irish annals invariably use the Latin term *gentiles*, or its Irish equivalent, *gennti*) rendered them more fearsome to Christian observers.

Sources of Raiding Bands

Much debate has focused on the likely source of the viking raids that struck Ireland's maritime zone from the end of the eighth century. The earliest attacks impacted severely on ecclesiastical sites in western Scotland, or in northern and eastern Ireland, which were subject to the sixth-century foundation of St. Columba on Iona. Record of these forays commences from 794, with reference to 'the devastation of all the islands of Britain by heathens' – which in all probability means the Scottish Isles. The following year, 795, Iona itself was attacked and then, coupled with a raid on the Isle of Skye, comes notice of viking activity closer to Ireland's coastline with the burning of Rechru. The identification of this site gave rise to some dispute in the past. Although Lambay (an island off Dublin featuring early Christian settlement) was formerly known as Rechru, its location seems out of line geographically with other sites targeted in this earliest phase of raiding. In recent decades, it has become widely accepted that the Rechru concerned was probably Rathlin off Co. Antrim, especially since excavations on the island have revealed an early Christian cemetery.

Decorated Viking-age iron sword hilt, no location.

It makes geographical sense that a sequence of raids should have progressed from Shetland and Orkney, via the Hebrides, to the north-east corner of Ireland. This progression was carried further in the later months of 795 when the vikings, it seems, sailed past Ireland's northern shores and down the west coast, raiding the islands of Inishmurray and Inishboffin. In 798, they made their way into the Irish Sea – striking at Inis Pátraic, thought to be St. Patrick's Island off

798 AD The burning of Inis Pátraic by the heathens, and the cattle tribute of the territories was taken, and the shrine of St. Do-chonna broken by them, and sea-incursions were also made by them both in Ireland and in Britain.

The Annals of Ulster. (Translation by the author.)

Viking remains from the Memorial Park Islandbridge burial ground.

Skerries, Co. Dublin. In the years following, there were further attacks on Iona itself (802 and 806), again on Inishmurray, and at Roscam on the Galway coast (807). The trail apparently followed by these raiders, by way of the Scottish Isles to Ireland, suggests a movement from Norway rather than from elsewhere in Scandinavia. Archaeological evidence, indeed, serves to confirm such a picture. In several regions of southern Norway, notably in Vestfold, viking graves have produced quantities of metal artefacts from the Irish Sea area, some of which seem to pre-date the time of historically-recorded raids. The sheer distance from Norway to Scotland, much less Ireland, and the apparent age of some of the insular objects when deposited in graves, has prompted speculation about 'intermediate bases' in the Faroe Islands and the Northern Isles of Scotland, and even about 'pre-viking' Scandinavian settlement in these parts.

In recent years, a consensus has emerged among archaeologists on the lack of evidence, before the mid-ninth century, for Scandinavian settlement in Scottish territories, even in the Northern Isles. It seems unlikely that there were 'intermediate bases' in any formal sense. There are, however, hints of contact; reindeer antler was imported into Shetland and Orkney and was used for comb-making on sites which appear to pre-date the viking period. Likewise, it has been suggested that the word *Péttar* (the Picts of northern Britain) had been borrowed into Old Norse by the eighth century. If there was occasional trade between Norway and the Northern Isles prior to 794 – or if Norwegians were, by agreement, fishing the waters of northern Scotland – the sheltering there of ships prior to embarking on viking expeditions need not have caused any great stir. The case, therefore, for 'harbours of convenience' along the way need not be dismissed. Orkney and Shetland were thinly populated and could scarcely have offered much resistance; besides, the inhabitants might willingly have supplied shelter and provisions to ships' crews with whose countrymen they already had a trading relationship. The alternative, that raiding parties sailed directly from Norway to Ireland and back without stopping on the way, appears less likely.

Carved dragonhead from the Oseberg ship.
Universitets Oldsaksamling, Oslo.

The Irish Experience

Condemnation by clerical observers of the ferocity of viking attacks was not without cause; nor were fears expressed by contemporary writers unfounded. Violence was certainly a feature of viking activity. Scandinavian skaldic poetry of later medieval date celebrates some of the more brutal actions of heroes from the Viking Age. The raiders who

Golden dawn shone forth . . . when this holy teacher, celebrating the holy sacrifice of the mass, stood before the sacred altar as a calf without blemish, a pleasing offering to God, to be sacrificed by the threatening sword . . . .
and after slaying with mad savagery the rest of the associates, they approached the holy father to compel him to give up the precious metals wherein lie the holy bones of St. Columba; . . . but the saint . . . [had been] trained to stand against the foe, and to arouse the fight, and [was] unused to yield. . . . Therefore the pious sacrifice was torn limb from limb.

Walafrid Strabo, *The Life of Blathmac*, 264–5.

The remains of the Nydam boat, from Schleswig. Schleswig-Holstein Landesmuseum.

struck Iona in 806 slew sixty-eight of the community. The construction
of a new Columban centre at Kells commenced the following year. In 825
and in 828, two prominent churchmen – Blathmac of Iona and
Temnén the venerable anchorite – met violent deaths at the hands of
viking raiders. An account of the death of Blathmac, a one-time
princely warrior turned monk who perished in an attempt to protect
the relics of St. Columba, is related by Walafrid Strabo of St. Gallen.
Apparently Walafrid, whose monastery had originally been an Irish
foundation, received a description of Blathmac's fate from Irish exiles,
and probably dramatised the account to some degree. It seems that
the vikings had attempted to bargain for the relic-shrine which, they
understood, was made of valuable metals. The stalwart custodian,
however, refused to yield and was, it is related, 'torn limb from limb'.
On this account it was postulated that Blathmac was slain according to
the 'blood-eagle' ritual. Lurid descriptions of 'blood-eagling' abound,
claiming that victims were hacked under both shoulder blades and their
arms, from the shoulders, forced into a form resembling eagles' wings.
Some Scandinavian historical tales from the *Heimskringla* appear to
corroborate these accounts, but these belong to the later middle ages and
were perhaps subject to other literary influences. Many scholars are

A Viking long ship mounting the river to Rouen.
(Le Petit Journal supplement 4 June 1911).

now of the view that ritual 'blood-eagling' was a Continental literary invention. Nonetheless, many victims were slaughtered by vikings and some may indeed have been tortured.

A balanced view of the Viking Age, however, must take account of the fact that by no means all attacks against church centres were carried out by Scandinavians. Nor were all viking attacks directed at ecclesiastical settlements. Even when they were, the intended target was not always church valuables. Human captives were a useful asset; depending on their status, they could be sold as slaves or held for ransom. The raid on Étar (probably Howth, near Dublin) in 821 may well have been motivated by slaving. According to the annals, a 'large prey of women' was taken – but whether this was a secular settlement or a convent is uncertain. In 824, a foray on an ecclesiastical site, this time the hermitage of Scellig Mhichíl (Skellig Rocks, Co. Kerry) resulted in the capture of one Étgal, who died in captivity. It is not expressly stated that Étgal was abbot of Scellig, but it seems clear that he was an individual of importance. In all probability, the viking party were holding him to ransom but their plan did not come to fruition; certainly there are later instances on record of individuals being held hostage for profit. Moreover, the Latin *Life of Findan of Rheinau* tells how this Irish monk, of Leinster origin, was captured by vikings with the connivance of an Irish king. He was later sold on to other viking owners, eventually escaping to make his career as a churchman on the Continent.

In the year 832 it is recorded that, within the space of a single month, three raids were launched against Armagh. Such attacks against an inland site indicate that vikings in Ireland had by this time the capacity to make cross-country forays – presumably with the use of horses. Furthermore, repetition of the venture three times suggests that the intended target was probably not valuables (which any competent group of pillagers would surely have seized on the first occasion!), but rather a renewable resource – either slaves or food. Viking bands are known to have engaged in hunting, and seals and porpoises were among their quarries. One party slaughtered porpoises on the coast of Ciannachta (between Balbriggan and Drogheda) in 828. The local population are unlikely to have welcomed foreign competition for a valuable natural resource; nine years later, a viking contingent active in the area was attacked by the men of Ciannachta and its chieftain, a man named Saxolb, was slain.

'Invasion' and Resistance

By the second third of the ninth century, however, the pattern of viking warfare in Ireland was changing. For three decades or so from 795, coastal raids by small seaborne forces seem to have been the norm. Then, from the 830s, a 'new phase' is characterised by larger fleets which penetrate up navigable rivers and plunder extensive inland areas. On the Continent, these years saw increased raiding by the Danes against trading hubs like Dorestadt and Quentovic, while river-borne forces made their way up such principal waterways as the Loire and the Seine to attack such major centres as Nantes and Paris. In Ireland, mainstream annals report higher levels of activity in the east and centre, in the valleys of the rivers Boyne, Liffey, Nore, Shannon and Brosna. To some degree, this geographical slant is a product of the surviving record; overall documentation is more detailed for these parts of the country. However other sources, including the 'annal section' of the twelfth-century propaganda tract *Cogadh Gáedhel re Gallaib* (The War of the Irish with the Foreigners) do not alter the picture significantly, while archaeological evidence datable to the ninth century creates a broadly similar impression. Presumably, viking raids would focus more on those parts of the country where agricultural resources were generally more abundant and major settlements (ecclesiastical or otherwise) most dense. It must be assumed that the end goal of the raiders was maximum profit.

Along with this intensified raiding from the 830s onwards, permanent bases were established by the vikings in areas which seemed to offer good potential for exploitation. For example, settlements were built on the Ile de Noirmoutier at the mouth of the Loire and on the Isle of Sheppey in the Thames estuary. In Ireland, defended camps of a type called *longphort* in the annals were established in 841 at Linn Duachaill (near Annagassan, Co. Louth) and – more significantly – at Duiblinn. This was the forerunner of the town of Dublin. However, while several examples of *longphoirt* are known from historical sources, definitive archaeological evidence for this settlement type remains elusive. In 1995, an argument was advanced that the *longphort* of Rothlabh (Hróðúlfr, Old Norse), destroyed by the Irish in 862, could be identified with a D-shaped enclosure known as Dunrally on the River Barrow, Co. Laois. The suggestion was met with considerable scepticism. Since then, however, attention has

Reconstruction of Viking long ship crossing the Atlantic to the
Chicago World's Fair 1888 (wood engraving, 1888).

been drawn to Athlunkard (Co. Limerick) where there is a similar enclosure. Here, the placename preserves the element *longphort*, and several viking age finds have been made in the vicinity. Comparisons have been made with another enclosure near Annagassan and with several sites in England. The debate seems set to continue.

The implication is that these *longphoirt* were, in the initial stages, bases from which to plunder their surrounding hinterlands. Before long, however, they evolved from mere protected harbours and stores for plunder into colonial settlements and emporia for trade. Grave-goods from the vicinity of Dublin, dateable to the ninth century, comprise not only weapons but implements of trade and commerce. Finds include smithing tools, shears, sickles and scales – along with spindle whorls and what appear to be needle cases, pointing to the presence of women. Apparently, at least some of Ireland's rural Scandinavian settlement dates to this initial phase of colonisation. Recent excavation at Cherrywood (south Co. Dublin) has revealed dwellings provisionally dated to the ninth century, one a classic Viking longhouse, and burials which again featured women.

Regarding Duiblinn itself, the precise location of the earliest settlement on the Liffey is another contentious issue. Viking burials have long been recognised a mile or so upriver, near the ford of Áth Cliath, where they probably formed two clusters around adjacent Early Christian sites at Kilmainham and Islandbridge, rather than a continuous cemetery as was once thought. However, clear evidence of occupation has not been found. Alternative sites proposed for the early *longphort* have included Usher's Island – now an extension of the quays, but once a dry area surrounded by river marsh. In the late 1990s, excavations in the Temple Bar/Essex Street area produced traces of settlement which certainly appear non-native – dating to the mid ninth-century, if not earlier, but seemingly continuing into the tenth century without a break. It is, therefore, possible that the original viking base of Duiblinn lay near the Liffey/ Poddle confluence, in what ultimately became the north-east sector of the town.

Getting agreement on the likely location of the early viking settlement has not been helped by uncertainty in identifying the ecclesiastical site of Duiblinn, which is mentioned twice in the annals. Some have suggested a large circular enclosure in the Whitefriar Street area, while others have looked a little further upriver. More recently, however, attention has focused on the church site of St. Michael le Pole, the name of which commemorates the 'pool' at the Poddle confluence. A question to be resolved is whether or not the placename 'Duiblinn' was restricted to the 'pool'. Elsewhere the term *linn* is used liberally to describe ponds, creeks and other such features – rather like the English term *water*, which can apparently mean anything from a lake to a stream to a sea-inlet. Perhaps 'Duiblinn' meant the Liffey estuary. A clearer understanding of such topographical matters, and of pre-existing settlement in the locality, is important in order to appreciate the context in which the Dublin colony was established.

Scholarship of recent years has shown that the Liffeyside settlement of the ninth century would not, according to most accepted sets of criteria, have constituted a town, much less a city; indeed it may even have had more than one focus. Be that as it may, it survived, grew, developed as a political entity and successfully exploited its borderline position between the overkingdoms of Uí Néill and Uí Dúnlainge. However, although the vikings successfully established colonies in Ireland during this period, and the level of hostilities greatly increased, they conquered no extensive territories. In England, half the country came under viking rule and a Danish dynasty ultimately secured control of the emerging monarchy. Historians have tried to explain the limited political achievement of the vikings in Ireland in terms of the country's political fragmentation, while invader numbers were assumed to be small. However, modern reassessment of political developments has shown that Ireland was not as fragmented as was once thought; powerful overking-ships had emerged which were capable of rising to quite a strong military challenge and which did so with more aggression than their English counterparts.

There came after that a great royal fleet into the north of Erinn, with Turgeis, who assumed the sovereignty of the foreigners of Erinn; and the north of Erinn was plundered by them and they spread themselves over Leth Chuinn.

There came now Turgeis . . . and brought a fleet upon Loch Rai and from thence plundered Midhe and Connacht; and Cluain mic Nois was plundered by him, and Cluain Ferta of Brenann, and . . . all the churches of Derg dheirc . . . .

It was in this year (i.e. 845) Turgeis was taken prisoner by Máel-Sechnaill; and he was afterwards drowned in Loch Uair.

Anonymous, 'Cogadh Gáedhel re Gallaib', paras 9, 11, 14, pp. 9, 13, 15.

Amongst the Irish kings of the mid-ninth century who helped to halt the viking incursions, Máel-Sechnaill son of Máel-ruanaid, Southern Uí Néill king of Tara, deserves particular mention. In 845, he captured and drowned one Turgesius (ON Thorgestr?), a chieftain whose marauding forces were wreaking havoc in the midlands. Turgesius features in *Cogadh Gáedhel re Gallaib* as a villainous oppressor of Ireland, before the Dál Cais kings came to power and – as they liked to claim – freed their country-men from subjection. How much influence this man may have wielded as a viking leader is not clear; but the very fact that his name is recorded in Irish annals suggests a perceived importance. It may not be coincidence that after his death the tide appears to have turned against the vikings. In 848, Máel-Sechnaill defeated the vikings at Forrach (near Skreen, Co. Meath), where seven hundred of them fell. That same year, in which the rulers of Munster and Leinster also achieved a signal victory over the Norsemen, Irish kings sent an embassy to the emperor of the Franks.

Settlements and Alliances

Viking raids declined in the latter part of the ninth century. *Cogadh Gáedhel re Gallaib* mentions a 'forty years rest', and much ink has been spilled in striving to date this period of respite in relation to a recog-nisable upsurge in hostilities in the early tenth century. The reality may well be that this 'rest' was never clearly defined in chronological terms; nor was it necessarily 'absolute' in quality. It merely expresses an awareness that viking aggression in Ireland during the later ninth century was generally less intense, and perhaps different in character. Various factors contributed to this change; the emergence of dissension among the vikings themselves, the gradual centralisation of political power in their homelands, the progressive integration of Scandinavian colonies into Ireland's political framework, and the diversion of energies into other theatres of activity.

The Irish annals note the appearance at Dublin in 851 of the *Dubgennti* ('Dark Heathens'). Many have interpreted this as meaning 'dark-haired foreigners' and equated these new arrivals with the Danes.

Table 1: Early kings of the Dublin Norsemen

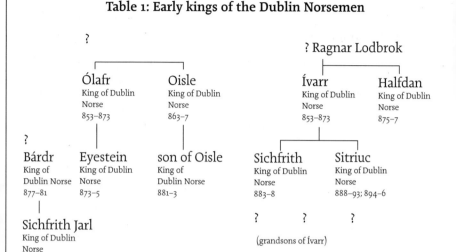

?			? Ragnar Lodbrok	
Ólafr King of Dublin Norse 853–873	**Oisle** King of Dublin Norse 863–7		**Ívarr** King of Dublin Norse 853–873	**Halfdan** King of Dublin Norse 875–7

?
Bárdr
King of
Dublin Norse
877–81

Eyestein
King of Dublin
Norse
873–5

son of Oisle
King of
Dublin Norse
881–3

Sichfrith
King of Dublin
Norse
883–8

Sitriuc
King of Dublin
Norse
888–93; 894–6

Sichfrith Jarl
King of Dublin
Norse
893–4

?   ?   ?

(grandsons of Ívarr)

However, dark hair is not especially a Danish characteristic. Perhaps the term merely describes incomers as opposed to established settlers; *dub* (dark, black) in the sense of young, fresh, in contrast to *finn* (fair, white), meaning old, hoary. In that sense, *Dubgennti* could equally apply to Danes intruding via England, or to a fresh Norwegian influx coming through the Scottish Isles. In any event, bitter fighting ensued between the newcomers and the *Finngaill*. Gradually, the situation stabilised with the intervention, from 853, of Ólafr (Amlaíb in Irish sources) and Ívarr, who appear to have been powerful Scandinavian magnates. Later sources, Scandinavian and Irish, make various claims regarding the identities of these men. Ólafr is said to have been a son of Gothfrith; he has been linked to the royal line of Vestfold, and it has even been suggested that his remains lie in a ship-burial at Gokstad, in southern Norway. It is believed that he was active in Scotland; certainly the mid-ninth century witnessed extensive Scandinavian settlement in the Northern Isles and in the Hebrides. Ívarr was supposedly a son of the Danish viking-king Ragnar Loðbrók, who was credited with many exploits in various parts

AD 866. In this year a heathen army took up their quarters in Thanet, and made peace with the people of Kent, and the people of Kent promised them money for the peace; and during the peace and the promise of money, the army stole itself away by night and ravaged all Kent eastward.

AD 871. In this year the army rode over Mercia into East Anglia, and took winter quarters at Thetford; and in that winter, King Eadmund fought against them, and the Danes gained the victory and slew the king, and subdued all that land, and destroyed all the monasteries which they came to. The names of the chiefs who slew the king were Ingvan and Ubba.

Benjamin Thorpe (ed.), *The Anglo-Saxon Chronicle*. London, 1861, ii, 59, 60.

of the Continent. The respective origins assigned to these allies may reflect the fact that Danish rule, at different times up to the eleventh century, extended over the Oslofjord region adjacent to Vestfold.

From the 850s, the Dublin settlement became the focus of a Scandinavian kingdom in Ireland. As early as 857, Ólafr and Ívarr were fighting in Munster against the viking magnate, Ketill Flatnef, who also claimed sway in the Hebrides. Before long, the two Dublin-based kings were deeply embroiled in Irish politics, supporting one Irish ruler against another. From 865, the Danish 'Great Army', in which Ívarr featured prominently, campaigned in England. This same period saw greatly increased viking activity in Francia; much of this was also Danish led, but probably featured Norwegian elements – including some from Ireland. This redirection of energies away from Ireland doubtless helped Irish kings to reverse many previous Scandinavian gains. In 866 Áed Finnliath,

Map 2: Ireland (9th–10th c)

AD 855. Around this time Rodolb came with his forces to invade Osraige. Cerball son of Dúnlang (sic = Dúngal) mobilised an army against them, and engaged them, and defeated the Northmen .... That rout was inflicted at Áth Muiceda [unlocated; in Ossory] .... Great indeed was the slaughter which was made there of the Northmen.

AD 858. A rout by Cerball son of Dúngal and by Ímar of the 'Foreign Irish' in Ara Tíre [barony of Owney and Arra, Co. Tipperary].

AD 860. Two fleets' companies of Norsemen came raiding into the territory of Cerball son of Dúngal.... and more than half of that host was killed there and the survivors fled to their ships. At Achad mic Erclaige [Agha, near Kilkenny city] this rout took place.

AD 861. A slaughter by Cerball son of Dúngal of the followers of Rodolb at Sliab Mairge [Slievemargy, bordering Cos. Kilkenny and Laois], and they were all killed except for a few of them who fled into the woods.

AD 862. A bloody slaughter was inflicted by Cerball son of Dúngal and Cennétig son of Gáethíne (i.e. the son of Cerball's sister) on the fleet of Rodolb, which a short time beforehand had come from Norway.

AD 863. A slaughter of the foreigners by Cerball son of Dúngal at Fertae Cairech [Fertagh, Co. Kilkenny], and they abandoned their booty.

Fragmentary Annals paras. 249, 263, 277, 281, 308, 310. Translation by the author, pp. 98, 104, 108, 110, 114.

Northern Uí Néill king of Ailech, gained a signal victory at Lough Foyle and proceeded to root out viking bases from the northern coasts. Even before this, considerable success had been achieved against vikings based in the Nore Valley by Cerball (d. 888) son of Dúngal, king of Osraige (Ossory). During the 850s and 860s, he defeated them in a series of engagements fought in the Munster marchlands. In 867, allies of Cerball made so bold as to sack a fortress of Ólafr at Clondalkin, within reach of Dublin.

From the early 870s, the Dublin kingdom began to experience difficulties. Ólafr disappears from the record; he may have returned to Norway to contest a kingship there. Ívarr, styled in the annals 'king of the

Norsemen of all Ireland and Britain', died in 873. His death signalled a contest for the control of Dublin, between Barith (ON Barðr) – a supporter of Ólafr – and Halfdan, a Danish or Oslofjord-Danish ruler from Northumbria, whom the Irish annals describe as 'king of the *Dubgennti*'. The intervention of the powerful Áed Finnliath ensured that Barith prevailed, at least for a time. The decades following, in which renewed raiding again swamped Francia, saw extensive secondary colonisation by Irish-based Scandinavians into the North Atlantic. The same period witnessed a further reduction in viking activity in Ireland, and the failure of this first Dublin kingdom.

No fewer than five dynasts, kinsmen of Ólafr and Ívarr, fell in internecine conflicts after comparatively brief reigns. When Sitriuc son of Ívarr was murdered by other Norsemen in 896, it appears there was no clear successor. Such dissension probably facilitated the sack of the Dublin settlement in 902 by an alliance of Irish kings from the eastern region. The annalist makes the dramatic claim that 'the heathens were driven from Ireland'. This hardly means that every colonist was uprooted from the Dublin district; clearly, intermarriage had already taken place between the settlers and the native Irish. Political and economic realities were far too complex to be tackled by 'ethnic cleansing'. Presumably only the rulers and their retainers were driven from the Dublin settlement. Surviving members of this elite sought refuge in England. Fifteen years later, when political circumstances had changed, some of them returned to establish a stronger kingship of Dublin.

AD 902. The expulsion of the heathens from Ireland, i.e. from the *longphort* of Dublin, by Máel-Finnia son of Flannacán with the men of Brega and by Cerball son of Muirecán with the Leinstermen, so that they abandoned a great number of their ships and escaped half-dead after having been wounded and defeated.

The Annals of Ulster. Translation by the author, 352.

Timeline: The 'Fury of the Northmen'

	Viking activity in Britain/ Continent	Viking activity in Ireland
775		
	'Dorsetshire incident' (787)	
	Attack on Lindisfarne (793)	Raid on Iona (795); Rechru burned
	'devastation of the islands of Britain'(794)	Raid on Inis Pátraic (798)
800	Attack on St. Philipert, France (799)	
	Harrying of Frisia (810)	
	Harrying of French coast (820)	Martyrdom of Blathmac (825)
825		
	Settlements on Isle de Noirmoutier and Isle of Sheppey (830s)	Raid on Armagh three times in one month (832)
		Inland fleets on Irish rivers (830s)
		Settlement at *Duiblinn* (841)
850		Máel-Sechnaill defeats vikings (848)
		Arrival of the *Dubgennti* (851)
		Arrival of Ólafr and Ívarr (853)
		Cerball battles vikings (850s, 860s)
	Great Army active in England (860s)	
		Áed Finnliath defeats vikings (866)
875		Ólafr disappears; Ívarr dies (873)
	Renewed raiding in France (870s, 880s)	
900		Viking rulers expelled from Dublin (902)

3. The 'Foreigners' and the Irish 9th–11th Centuries

New Scandinavian Kingdoms in Ireland

The fresh influx of Scandinavian colonists into Ireland in the early tenth century, and the political expansion that followed, have attracted much attention from historians and archaeologists alike. This renewal of Norse interest in Ireland, motivated in part, perhaps, by the closing off of other avenues, occurred against a background of increased viking activity in the Irish Sea area. An alliance of three magnates came to take control of this expansion. Described as brothers – Ragnall, Sitriuc, and Gothfrith – they were said to have been grandsons of Ívarr, although their exact connection with the king of Dublin who died in 873 is unclear. The ruling elite of Dublin, expelled in 902, had fled to the north-west coast of England; the Cuerdale Hoard from Lancashire is thought to represent part of their wealth. It is distinctly possible that these Norsemen from Ireland linked up with Danish dynasts whose assets included the remnants of the 'Great Army' which had returned from the Continent in the 890s. Dublin, from its early days, had been of considerable interest to the Danes (or Oslofjord Danes) of Northumbria; Halfdan, the alleged brother of Ívarr who had contested control of the settlement with Barith in the 870s, was one of their number.

Ragnall (Røgnvald) moved in 914 to attack the Isle of Man and defeat another *jarl* named Barith (Bárðr) to gain control there. Viking settlement in Man, it seems, was still a recent development at that time. Some graves there, it has been claimed, date to the ninth century, but recent reassessment would see most of these, including the ship-burials, as dating to the late ninth or early tenth century. Meanwhile new viking fleets were landing in the south of Ireland – especially at Loch Dá Chaech (Waterford Haven), a base from which raids extended into many parts of Munster and Leinster. The following decade saw more focus on the northern, and especially north-eastern, coasts, and the loughs of Carlingford and Strangford and the Foyle estuary

Model boat, possibly a child's toy, carved in wood, from Dublin Fishamble St. excavations.

3 cm

became zones of conflict. It is clear from the annals that these new arrivals were pagan; indeed viking graves in this north-eastern region, including Ballywillin (Co. Antrim) and Ballyholme (Co. Down) which some interpret as boat-burials, may relate to these early tenth-century incursions and so parallel the better-known boat-burials in the Isle of Man. Meanwhile, in 917, Ragnall led his alliance to Ireland and seized control of the operations at Waterford Haven.

AD 917. Sitriuc grandson of Ívarr, with his fleet, landed at Cenn Fuait in the east of Leinster.

A hosting of the Uí Néill of the south and north by Niall son of Áed king of Ireland, to the land of Munster to fight against the heathens. He halted on the 22nd August at Tobar Glethrach in Mag Femin .... Niall remained after that twenty nights encamped against the heathens. He sent word to the Leinstermen that they should attack the longphort from a distance. The battle of Cenn Fuait was broken upon them by Sitriuc grandson of Ívarr, in which fell five hundred more or less..... Sitriuc grandson of Ívarr entered into Dublin.

The Annals of Ulster. Translation by the author, 366.

A key event in the establishment of this new regime in Ireland was a battle fought that same year at Cenn Fuait. The site of this engagement was traditionally identified with Confey (near Leixlip, Co. Dublin), but in recent years reconsideration has focused on the landings at Waterford, and a location has been sought in that area. However, the *Annals of Ulster* place the arrival of Sitriuc at Cenn Fuait 'in eastern Leinster'; his fleet could certainly have navigated the Liffey as far as Confey. The army of the king of Tara, before calling upon the Leinstermen to help, advanced as far as Mag Femin; there was a plain of that name in south County Meath. They urged the Leinstermen to attack the foreign encampment 'from a distance'. In the ensuing encounter, the Leinstermen were routed with the loss of more than five hundred men; all of the named casualties belonged to north-Leinster dynasties. As a direct outcome of the contest, Sitriuc gained control of Dublin. This would be a likely result of a battle fought in the Liffey plain, rather than in Waterford. Almost two years later, the Norsemen won the important battle of Islandbridge, near Dublin, in

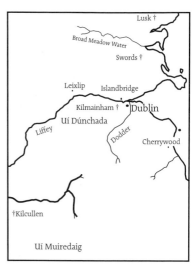

Dyfflinarskiri – regional kingdom of Dublin (late 10thc)

which the king of Tara, Niall Glúndub, fell. The restored Scandinavian kingship of Dublin was now secure.

Although the decades that followed saw Dublin reach the apex of its political strength, the new ruling dynasty – which had retained a base in York – seems to have been more concerned with maintaining its hold on the Scandinavian kingship of Northumbria. Ragnall betook himself to York in 918, and defeated invaders from Scotland on the banks of the Tyne. He died suddenly in 921 and was immediately succeeded by Sitriuc, leaving the less prestigious kingship of Dublin to the third brother, Gothfrith (reigned 921–34). He was in turn followed by his son Ólafr (reigned 934–41). During these years, the dynasty expanded its Irish interests, acquiring influence over other emerging Scandinavian settlements, notably at Waterford and Limerick. It appears that bases at these locations, which had existed for several decades, were viewed as centres for potential expansion by a new generation of royals. In the 930s, the settlement at Limerick came under the control of Haraldr, a ruler of the Western Isles, seemingly with the support of his kinsman

Ólafr Gothfrithsson, king of Dublin. Meanwhile Dublin itself gradually increased in status, becoming the focus of an overkingdom which extended its authority mainly at the expense of north Leinster dynasties.

Dublin and Power-Politics

The core-territory of Dublin (*Dyflinarskiri* of later Scandinavian sources) appears restricted, probably because of the small numbers of colonists. The scarcity of Scandinavian placenames in Ireland, compared to northern England or to Caithness and the Scottish Isles, has often been noted. They are overwhelmingly coastal; Leixlip (*Laks-laup*; 'salmon-leap'), about nine miles upriver from Dublin, is one of only a small number of inland examples. Placenames in this area suggest possible Scandinavian settlement; attention has been drawn to Barnhall, south of Leixlip. Ravensdale, about two miles to the northeast, may be another case for consideration. Even where it is possible to locate Scandinavian dwelling sites, it appears that settlement did not, in all cases, correspond with political control. There is archaeological evidence for viking occupation on the island of Beginish (Co. Kerry) – far away from any Norse-Irish political centre. Nor did the colonists necessarily displace the local population; on the contrary, there are signs of integration. It can be inferred from the annals that at various times in the tenth century the kings of Dublin, whose heartland lay probably between the Broad Meadow Water and the Dodder, with coastal extensions for about ten miles to the north and south and upriver as far as Leixlip, acted as overlords within northern Leinster.

Throughout most of the tenth century, as the historical record testifies, Ireland experienced what might be described as 'viking aggression'. Attacks on ecclesiastical settlements continued, but they were less frequent and focused almost exclusively on high-profile sites which had close connections with Irish ruling families. Such actions, therefore, it seems clear, were politically motivated. The Scandinavians of Ireland gradually fitted into the framework of Irish politics, siding with one native dynasty against another. Indeed, the emergence from

High Street excavations undertaken by Brendan O'Riordan, who pioneered the rediscovery of Viking Dublin.

944 of Congalach son of Máel-mithig, who belonged to a politically marginal branch of Uí Néill and yet managed to attain the kingship of Tara, was due, at least in part, to support from the Dubliners. While some Norse military ventures of this era undoubtedly served self-interest, with much wealth taken and large numbers of captives (probably for the slave market), other attacks can be interpreted in the light of inter-dynastic warfare. Several major ecclesiastical centres in the Uí Néill sphere of influence were raided between *c.*920 and mid-century,

AD 921. The invasion of Ard Macha on the 4th of the Ides [10th] November by the foreigners of Dublin, i.e. by Gothfrith grandson of Ívarr, with his army on the Saturday before the feast of St. Martin, and the oratories were spared by him, with their complement of celibate clergy and sick persons, and likewise the church – except for a few dwellings there which were destroyed through carelessness.

The Annals of Ulster. Translation by the author, 366.

notably Kells, Clonmacnois and Armagh; although when Armagh was first plundered by the new rulers of Dublin in 921, they spared the prayer-houses and the shelters of the sick. During the same decades, some north Leinster foundations also suffered attacks, including Kildare and Kilcullen. Nor were the Scandinavian territories left untouched: in 938, Donnchad grandson of Máel-Sechnaill, king of Tara, plundered the foreigners 'from Áth Truisten to Áth Cliath' (from near Castledermot, Co. Kildare, to Dublin) which implies that the greater part of the kingdom of Uí Dúnlainge (see map p. 49) was under tribute to the Norsemen at that time. In 944, Donnchad's successor Congalach son of Máel-mithig, who occasionally used Norse forces, sacked the settlement of Dublin itself.

In the late 930s–940s, however, Ireland's principal Scandinavian dynasty experienced something of a crisis. In 937, striving to preserve their kingship of York against the expanding power of Athelstan, king of the English, they had suffered a costly defeat at Brunanburh in northern England. This probably left them vulnerable to offensives from Irish rulers. The several short reigns and regencies which followed the death of Ólafr Gothfrithsson in 941 hardly helped political continuity. Successes during these years were offset by the sacking of Dublin in 944, and by another heavy defeat inflicted four years later by Congalach son of Máel-mithig. Ólafr son of Sitriuc, known in Irish sources as Amlaíb Cuarán, had succeeded to the kingship of Dublin in 945, but left to pursue ambitions in York, leaving his brother Gothfrith at home as regent. The latter's campaign of 951, in which he sacked Kells and other Uí Néill ecclesiastical sites, went a considerable distance towards restoring the prestige – and wealth – of Dublin. However in 953, as the situation in York continued to deteriorate, Amlaíb abandoned the effort in England. Thereafter, the political ambitions of the Dublin rulers narrowed in scope, although they retained an important stake in the Irish Sea area – especially in relation to Man and the Isles.

From his return to Dublin in 953, Amlaíb Cuarán fitted more comfortably than his predecessors into the role of *rí mórtuaithe*, or ruler of a sub-provincial kingdom in the Irish sense. His sobriquet *Cuarán* may allude to a 'sandal', suggesting that he was inaugurated in

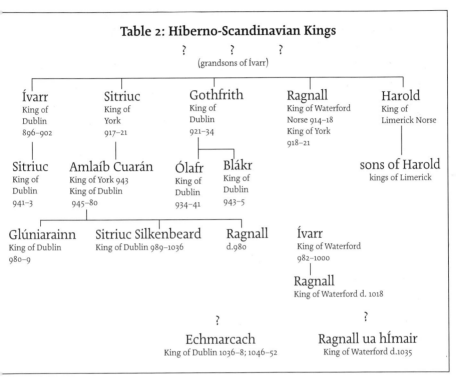

Table 2: Hiberno-Scandinavian Kings

?   ?   ?
(grandsons of Ívarr)

Ívarr
King of
Dublin
896–902

Sitriuc
King of
York
917–21

Gothfrith
King of
Dublin
921–34

Ragnall
King of Waterford
Norse 914–18
King of York
918–21

Harold
King of
Limerick Norse

Sitriuc
King of
Dublin
941–3

Amlaíb Cuarán
King of York 943
King of Dublin
945–80

Ólafr
King of
Dublin
934–41

Blákr
King of
Dublin
943–5

sons of Harold
kings of Limerick

Glúniarainn
King of Dublin
980–9

Sitriuc Silkenbeard
King of Dublin 989–1036

Ragnall
d.980

Ívarr
King of Waterford
982–1000

Ragnall
King of Waterford d. 1018

?

Echmarcach
King of Dublin 1036–8; 1046–52

?

Ragnall ua hÍmair
King of Waterford d.1035

accordance with Irish custom; as part of the enkinging ceremony, it was often the practice to place a shoe or sandal on the foot of the new king, so that he might walk in the footsteps of his predecessors. There is evidence that he was a patron of Irish literature; the distinguished poet Cináed ua hArtacáin composed a praise-poem in his honour. Amlaíb married Gormlaith, daughter of Murchad king of Uí Dúnlainge. She was the mother of his son Sitriuc – the future King Sitriuc Silkenbeard of Dublin. It also appears that Amlaíb was baptised a Christian – although this may have been due to pressure from Edmund, king of the West Saxons, with whom he concluded a peace during his adventures in England.

There are hints that the cult of St. Columba gained popularity in Dublin from the late tenth century; Sord Coluim Cille (Swords), which lay within the Dublin 'core area', is first mentioned in the annals at 994 when, significantly, it was burned by Máel-Sechnaill son of Domnall, king of Tara. The implication is that the site, by then, had Dublin dynastic connections. It would, of course, be a bold step to suggest that Swords, as a Columban site, owed its existence to Amlaíb. Nonetheless, it is curious that he died in 981 as a pilgrim on Iona. If this annalistic report can be trusted, the wheel had, in a sense, come full circle, with a Hiberno-Norse king ending his days in penance at the foundation of St. Columba, attacks on which had – from an Irish perspective – heralded the opening of the Viking Age.

An important development of Amlaíb Cuarán's reign was the beginning of the process whereby Ireland's Scandinavian settlements gradually assumed an urban character. While Dublin (arguments about the exact location of the *longphort* aside) existed from the 840s, present-day scholars are in general agreement that the early settlement, although it outgrew the role of military camp, did not meet the criteria for an urban centre. It seems that it became a focus for commerce – and to a certain extent for craft industry – at an early stage, mirroring the trading emporium of Kaupang in Norway and apparently was a seat of kingship, but there is no indication, at this stage, of an internal administration. Presumably, urban status was achieved only by degrees.

As our understanding of the archaeological record improves, it is clear that various 'urban functions' can be discerned only from the second half of the tenth century or later. The earliest defensive embankments, forerunners of the town walls, can be dated to about this time – as well as a formal urban layout with houses, situated within plots, lined along streets. These innovations imply planning, as does the apparent 'zoning' of industries whereby crafts are concentrated in particular areas. Overall, it is tempting to view such developments as an outcome of the return in 953 of Amlaíb

Amlaíb of Áth Cliath (Dublin) the hundred-strong
who gained the kingship in Benn Étair
I bore off from him as price of my song
a horse of the horses of Achall

Cináed ua hArtacáin, poem on Achall
Gwynn (ed.), *The Metrical Dindshenchas*.
Cináed flourished in the second half of the 10thc.

from York, where he would have had experience of a 'real' town. The reign of his son Sitriuc Silkenbeard witnessed the attainment of further urban functions – a coin mint by the 990s, and a cathedral, making Dublin a centre of religious administration, some three decades later.

Irish Overlordship of the Scandinavian Kingdoms

The era of Amlaíb Cuarán coincided with the gradual shrinking of Hiberno-Scandinavian military and political power in Ireland. Perhaps the single most influential factor in this decline was the emergence in Munster of a new dynasty – the Dál Cais. In 967, Mathgamain son of

> ... they marched that night until morning ... until they had entered the fort .... and the fort was sacked by them after that. They carried off their jewels and their best property, and their saddles beautiful and foreign; their gold and their silver; their beautifully woven cloth of all colours and of all kinds; their satins and silken cloth pleasing and variegated, both scarlet and green, and all sorts of cloth in like manner. They carried away their soft, youthful, bright, matchless girls; their blooming silk-clad young women; and their active, large and well formed boys. The fort and the good town they reduced to a cloud of smoke and to red fire afterwards.
>
> A twelfth-century version of the sack of Limerick by Dál Cais, 967 AD, 70.
> *Cogadh Gáedhel re Gallaib*, paras 9, 11, 14; pp. 79, 81.

Cennétig of Dál Cais, who had already taken the prestigious kingship of Cashel, moved against the Norse of Limerick – now ruled by sons of the above-mentioned Haraldr – and defeated them at Sulchóit (Solohead, Co. Tipperary). The sons of Haraldr were driven from Limerick, and Mathgamain despoiled the settlement. An account of the plunder taken is found in *Cogadh Gáedhel re Gallaib* (composed to glorify later Dál Cais rulers) where it is claimed that great quantities of jewels and silks fell into the hands of Mathgamain. Be that as it may, it was his younger brother and successor, the illustrious Brian Bóruma, who reaped the real benefits. It seems that Brian, from an early stage in his career, appreciated the Irish Sea context in which the Hiberno-Scandinavians operated, and exploited growing factionalism amongst the Norse ruling elite.

In 974, when the sons of Haraldr (whose family dominated the Western Isles) seized Ívarr, now king of the Limerickmen, presumably in an effort to regain control of the settlement, Brian opted for a bold political gamble. Three years later, after Ívarr had escaped from captivity, Brian attacked his fortress on Scattery Island (in the Shannon Estuary) and killed him along with his two sons. The Limerick settlement was now firmly under the control of Dál Cais. In 984, Brian marched to Waterford and met with the sons of Haraldr there. Together, they plotted to attack Dublin by land and sea. After some initial moves, these ambitious plans had to be shelved when rebellions broke out in Munster – occupying Brian's energies for several years. Nonetheless, it seems that by this time he already saw Dublin as a key factor in any attempt to extend his political dominance from *Leth Moga* (the southern half of Ireland) into *Leth Cuinn* (the northern half).

Meanwhile, Dublin's latest effort to flex its muscles in the east-midlands had brought the Hiberno-Norsemen into direct conflict with another major dynasty, the Uí Néill, whose overking was Máel-Sechnaill son of Domnall. In 980, a year before the death of Amlaíb, Máel-Sechnaill defeated the Dublin army in the important battle of Tara. Then, in 989, he effectively dismissed Amlaíb's eldest son and successor, Glúniarann, by sacking Dublin and placing the town under heavy tribute. Amongst the prizes taken on this occasion were valuable heirlooms of the Scandinavian kingship of Dublin, including the so-called 'sword of Carlus' and the 'collar of Tomrar'. This achievement, celebrated by bards of Máel-Sechnaill's own day, found echo in the early-modern songs of Thomas Moore, who called on the 'men of Erin' to remember the days 'when Malachy (Máel-Sechnaill) wore the collar of gold which he won from the proud invader'. It is possible that the tribute now imposed on Dublin, an ounce of gold for every household, influenced the decision of the new king, Sitriuc, to mint coins. However, it is widely agreed that more strictly commercial considerations were foremost; it was probably realised by about 995 that dependence on imported coinage from England and from the Arab world was no longer a viable option.

By the 990s, Brian Bóruma was strong enough to openly challenge the long-standing claims of the Uí Néill kings of Tara to political dominance in Ireland. The Dál Cais dynasty, having secured its overlordship of Munster and with the Hiberno-Norsemen of Limerick and Waterford firmly under its control, was strongly placed to wrest a compromise from Máel-Sechnaill. In 997, a royal meeting at Clonfert resulted in major concessions to Brian Bóruma: he was acknowledged by Máel-Sechnaill as the dominant force in southern Ireland. Two years later, a rebellion by a faction of the Uí Dúnlainge dynasty in northern Leinster, in alliance with the men of Dublin, gave Brian an excuse to

> AD 999. A hosting by Brian, king of Cashel, to Glenn Máma and there came the foreigners of Dublin to attack him, along with the Leinstermen; and they were defeated ....
> Brian proceeded afterwards into Dublin, and Dublin was plundered by him.
>
> AD 1000. The foreigners returned to Dublin and gave hostages to Brian.
>
> The Annals of Ulster. Translation by the author, 428.

move against the Hiberno-Scandinavian kingdom. Just after Christmas 999, he defeated a combined Leinster-Dublin force at Glenn Máma, and followed up with a thorough sack of Dublin on New Year's Day 1000.

As with the earlier plunder of Limerick, the twelfth-century *Cogadh Gáedhel re Gallaib* alludes to great wealth captured by the Dál Cais army. Of greater significance, however, is the fact that the king of Dublin, Sitriuc, fled from the town and was reinstated to his kingship only by the direct intervention of Brian. The Hiberno-Scandinavians were now bound more tightly than before under Irish lordship. Also, the Munster overking had now obtained a foothold in *Leth Cuinn* through dominance of Dublin, whose close connections with Man and the Isles he presumably aimed to exploit.

The years that followed saw Brian increase the Hiberno-Norse forces under his command. Confident that he could now disregard the pre-

Brian Boru before the battle of Clontarf; from D'Alton's History of Ireland.

viously agreed partition of Ireland, he proceeded against Máel-Sechnaill – this time with Dublin troops in his train. In an unprecedented development, in 1003, he obtained the submission of Máel-Sechnaill. This was the first time that a king of Tara had yielded the notional supremacy within Ireland to a political rival. Certainly the most powerful Irish king of his day, Brian made great capital of the discomfiture of the Uí Néill. When he visited Armagh in 1005, and made a generous donation to the church of St. Patrick, the (admittedly partisan) scribe who recorded the event styled him *Imperator Scotorum*, 'Emperor of the Irish'. It is widely acknowledged that Brian played a major part in advancing the notion of a high-kingship of Ireland; an assessment of his achievement in this

The small farms, bare mountains and narrow fjords of Norway.

Modern reconstruction of a long house at Trelleborg.

Reconstructed Viking boats have brought new insights into the ancient voyages across the northern seas, to Ireland, Iceland and even North America.

Slave chain
Human skull and chain for restraining a slave: relics of the major trade in slaves which the Vikings established in Ireland.

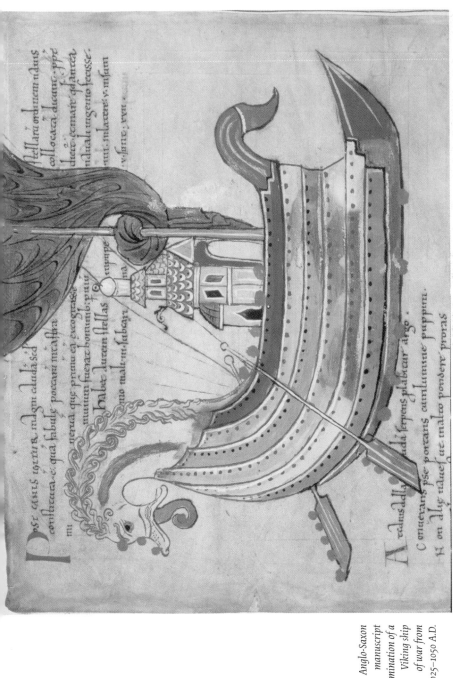

Anglo-Saxon manuscript illumination of a Viking ship of war from c.1025–1050 A.D.

Overhead view of Temple Bar, excavation, Dublin.

Temple Bar excavation.

Thistle brooch from Winetavern St. dig. Such items seem to have been a regular trade in Viking Dublin.

Items of amber, imported into Dublin from the Baltic. From Temple Bar dig, Dublin.

Legends of the northern seas (1): St. Brendan and the great fish Jasconius.
Woodcut by Anton Sorg (Augsburg, 1476)

(2): 'Leif Eriksson Discovers America'. Leif Ericson sights coast of Labrador around 1000.
Painting Christian Krohg, Norway. Nasjonalgalleriet, Oslo.

Reconstruction of turf longhouse at L'Anse aux Meadows, a Scandinavian colonial site in Newfoundland, Canada.

Carving in interior of Borgund stave church.

The Lewis Chessmen, carved from walrus ivory brought from the northern Arctic seas:

(top) complete set, (bottom) the knight piece.

These are among the most attractive of surviving Viking works of art.

regard would be a major task, and cannot be attempted here. However, for the rest of his reign he strove to make his claim to overlordship of Ireland a political reality. In the process, he campaigned widely, especially against the rulers of the north and north-west, and made extensive use of Hiberno-Scandinavian troops and fleets.

It is ironic that Brian, who had furthered his political prospects by exploiting Norse dynastic factions linked to the Hebrides, owed his ultimate downfall to Scandinavians from the north Irish Sea and from the Northern Isles of Scotland. In 1013, the Uí Dúnlainge ruler Máelmórda, whom Brian himself had appointed to a kingship of Leinster, rebelled against him. This man's sister Gormlaith, an estranged wife of Brian, who had also once been married to Amlaíb Cuarán and was the mother of Sitriuc Silkenbeard, is represented in later accounts as a major instigator of the conflict. She is credited with having persuaded her brother and her son of the importance of sourcing assistance from overseas. In the event, the Leinster-Dublin alliance attracted support from the Isle of Man and, perhaps more importantly, from Orkney – a *jarldom* which had close links

---

A king from Ireland called Sigtrygg was also there (in Orkney). He was the son of Olaf Kvaran. His mother was called Kormlod; she was endowed with great beauty … but … she was utterly wicked. She had been married to a king called Brian, but now they were divorced. Kormlod was … so filled with hate against him after their divorce that she wished him dead ….

Kormlod kept urging her son Sigtrygg to kill King Brian. For that purpose, she sent him to Earl Sigurd to ask for support ….

Sigtrygg sailed south to Ireland and told his mother that the earl had joined forces with them … She was pleased at this, but said that they would have to amass an even larger force. Sigtrygg asked where they could expect to get that. Kormlod replied 'There are two vikings lying off the Isle of Man with thirty ships, and they are so formidable that no-one can withstand them. They are called Ospak and Brodir. Go and meet them, and spare nothing to induce them to join you ….'

A twelfth/thirteenth-century Icelandic version of the prelude to the Battle of Clontarf (1014 AD). *Njal's Saga*, 342, 344.
Reproduced by permission of Penguin Books Ltd.

So these battalions were arranged and disposed in the following manner; the foreigners and the Leinstermen placed in the front of the murderous foreign Danes (sic) under Brodar, Earl of Caer Ebroc, chieftain of the Danes ... and the nobles of the foreigners of Western Europe, from Lochlann westwards, along with them. A line of one very great strong battalion was formed of all the foreigners of Dublin, and it was placed after the above, that is after the Danes. At their head were Dubgall son of Amlaíb, and Gilla-Ciaráin son of Glún-Iarainn son of Amlaíb ....

A twelfth-century Irish version of the Battle of Clontarf (1014 AD)
Cogadh Gáedhel re Gallaib, para. 94; 163–5.

However, now, they continued in battle-array and fighting from sunrise to evening ... and the tide had come to the same place again at the close of the day, when the foreigners were defeated; and the tide had carried away their ships from them, so that they had not at the last any place to fly to, but into the sea ....
An awful rout was made of the foreigners and of the Leinstermen, so that they fled simultaneously ... and the foreigners were drowned in great numbers in the sea ....

A twelfth-century Irish version of the Battle of Clontarf (1014 AD)
Cogadh Gáedhel re Gallaib, 191–3.

... the attendant perceived a party of the foreigners approaching them. The Earl Brodar was there, and two warriors along with him. 'There are people coming towards us here' said the attendant. 'Woe is me, what manner of people are they?' said Brian. 'A blue stark naked people' said the attendant. 'Alas' said Brian, 'they are the foreigners of the armour, and it is not to do good to thee that they come' ....
Brodar then turned round, and appeared with a bright, gleaming, trusty battle-axe in his hand, with the handle set in the middle of it. When Brian saw him he gazed at him, and gave him a stroke with his sword, and cut off his left leg at the knee, and his right leg at the foot. The foreigner dealt Brian a stroke which cleft his head utterly; and Brian killed the second man that was with Brodar, and they fell mutually by each other.

A twelfth-century Irish version of the death of Brian Bóruma (1014 AD)
Cogadh Gáedhel re Gallaib, 203.

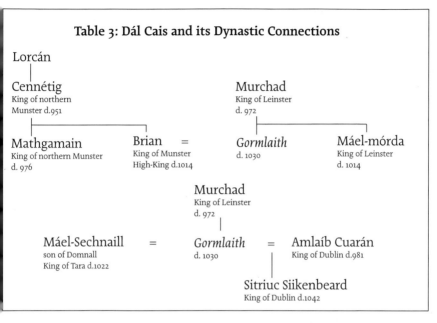

Table 3: Dál Cais and its Dynastic Connections

Lorcán

Cennétig
King of northern
Munster d.951

Murchad
King of Leinster
d. 972

Mathgamain
King of northern Munster
d. 976

Brian   =
King of Munster
High-King d.1014

Gormlaith
d. 1030

Máel-mórda
King of Leinster
d. 1014

Murchad
King of Leinster
d. 972

Máel-Sechnaill
son of Domnall
King of Tara d.1022

=

Gormlaith
d. 1030

=

Amlaíb Cuarán
King of Dublin d.981

Sitriuc Siikenbeard
King of Dublin d.1042

with an emerging Norwegian monarchy. It is possible that, to some degree, the plans of Máelmórda and Sitriuc meshed with even more ambitious agendas – as the ruling dynasty of Trøndelag progressed towards a centralised kingship of Norway (and, perhaps, sought to consolidate Norwegian influence in the Irish Sea area), while a Danish dynasty under Cnut established itself in England.

Be that as it may, the presence at Clontarf of Islesmen, who for the authors of *Cogadh Gáedhel re Gallaib* were 'the foreigners of the Western World', was enough to frustrate the forces of Dál Cais. The ensuing battle, fought on Good Friday 1014, is enshrined both in Irish and Norse saga. The outcome for the Munstermen could be described as a 'pyrrhic victory'; they held the field, but at enormous cost. The fallen included a number of Dál Cais dynasts, including the ageing Brian. Later propagandists contrived to have him die a martyr's death, slain while praying in a tent, but this is almost certainly a motif borrowed from English or Continental literature. Of greater importance than the precise manner of his death is that his removal from the scene brought

an immediate end to the personal political supremacy he had established. His son and successor, Donnchad, struggled for decades to
maintain Dál Cais dominance within Munster.

This contraction of Dál Cais power, however, brought only short-
term benefit to the Dublin Norsemen. The collapse of Munster control
over Leinster also weakened Uí Dúnlainge and facilitated the re-
emergence of the once prominent dynasty of Uí Cheinnselaig. Its ruler,
Diarmait mac Máele-na-mbó, having asserted his authority as overking
of Leinster, moved against Dublin in 1052 and expelled its king,
Echmarcach, seemingly a nephew of his predecessor Sitriuc. Having
first experimented with a Norse regent, Diarmait took the bold step of
installing his own son Murchad as king of Dublin. The Uí Cheinnselaig
rulers appear to have been more innovative in their approach to Irish
Sea politics; perhaps they learned from the earlier experiences of Dál
Cais. In any event, Murchad son of Diarmait took the initiative in 1061
and invaded the Isle of Man, driving the hapless Echmarcach to the
Rhinns of Galloway. At least for a time, then, they had managed to
twist an important link in the chain of Irish Sea alliances.

Until Diarmait's death in battle in 1072 (fighting, it appears, to
defend his Dublin realm against Uí Néill), his dominance of the
Hiberno-Scandinavians remained unchallenged. Small wonder that in
some annal accounts he is acclaimed not only as overlord of *Leth Moga*
(southern half of Ireland), but as suzerain of Britain (a pretentious
reference to his having acted as protector to the Welsh rulers of
Gwynned) and of *Inse Gall* – the Hebrides. The connections between
Dublin and the Isles, further exploited by Diarmait's successors as
overlords of *Leth Moga*, including the Ua Briain kings of Munster,
endured at least until the intervention of the Anglo-Normans in 1170.
The last century of Dublin's existence as a political unit in its own right
witnessed much political contest, with Manx and Hebridean elements
playing a part. However, the pattern established by Diarmait mac
Máele-na-mbó was maintained; although a Hiberno-Scandinavian
dynasty of local rulers emerged in the twelfth century, Dublin
remained under the control of Irish kings.

Timeline: The 'Foreigners' and the Irish		
	Viking activity in Britain/ Continent	Viking activity in Ireland
900	'grandsons of Ívarr' take Isle of Man (914)	'grandsons of Ívarr' defeat Uí Néill at Cenn Fuait; control Dublin (917); 'grandsons of Ívarr' defeat Uí Néill at Islandbridge (919)
925	Settlement of Normandy (920s)	Donnchad king of Tara plunders territories of the Dubliners (938)
	Scandinavians of England defeated at *Brunanburh* (937)	
950	Amlaíb Cuarán abandons York (953)	Amlaíb Cuarán king of Dublin (945)
		Dál Cais capture Limerick (967)
975	Economic difficulties in Scandinavia Birka abandoned (*c.*975)	Amlaíb Cuarán dies on Iona (981)
	Renewed raiding in England (980s)	Battle of Tara: defeat of Dublin (988)
1000		Brian Bóruma sacks Dublin (1000) Brian Bóruma high king (1003)
	Cnut of Denmark king of England (1016)	Battle of Clontarf; death of Brian (1014)
1025	Cnut takes control of Norway (1028) Norwegian royalty flee to Russia	Sitriuc founds cathedral (1028)
1050		Last independent king of Dublin expelled by Diarmait (1052)
	Haraldr Harðráði king of Norway launches invasion of England (1066)	Death of Diarmait (1072)
1075		

North Atlantic Seaways and Irish Hermit-Settlers

The late eighth century Scandinavian migrations in the direction of Britain and Ireland, which marked the effective beginning of the 'Viking Age', presumably proceeded via Shetland and Orkney to the north coast of Scotland, before turning westwards towards the Hebrides. The Northern Isles of Scotland were populated, before the dawn of history, by Picts whose language included (or absorbed) Celtic elements. Orkney preserves the Celtic name *Orcades* and, with Shetland, is rich in Pictish archaeological remains.

Both groups of islands were occupied by a small scattering of Irish religious hermits. From the sixth century onwards, these ascetics had gradually extended a chain of eremetical settlement up through the Hebrides to the Northern Isles. Adomnán, abbot of Iona, refers to Irish clerics on the northern peripheries of Scotland in his late seventh-

---

When this Cormac was travelling on the ocean for the third time . . . His ship had been driven with full sails by a steady wind from the south for fourteen summer days and nights, so that a straight course brought them to an area under the most northerly skies. They reckoned that they had passed beyond the range of human exploration, and had reached a place from which they might not be able to return.

There it happened, after the tenth hour of the fourteenth day . . . the whole sea was covered with deadly loathsome little creatures. They struck with horrible force against . . . the sides of the boat . . . and the pressure of them was so great that it was thought they would pierce the skin-covering . . . . These creatures (as those who were present afterwards described) were about the size of frogs, but exceedingly troublesome because they had spines, though they did not fly but merely swam.

Adomnán of Iona, *Life of St. Columba*, ii, § 42; 197.
Reproduced by permission of Penguin Books.
Cormac, who belonged to the lineage of Uí Liatháin, was a member of the Iona community who subsequently(early 7thc) settled at Durrow (Co. Offaly). Adomnán (d. 704) was writing in the 690s.

century 'Life of St. Columba'. A number of locations preserve the term *papa* as a placename-element. The Scandinavians called Irish eremites *papar*, from the Old Irish *popa* (in turn from the Latin *papa*), meaning 'father'. Orkney includes the small islands of Papa Stronsay and Papa Westray, and Shetland has Papa Stour and Papil in Burra.

These early clerics have left little impression in the archaeological record, but some remains are known, especially in Shetland. There are a few sculptured stones, including that at Papa Stronsay and a particularly fine example known as 'The Monk's Stone' at Papil in Burra, while inscriptions in the Irish *ogham* alphabet have come to light at Ninnian's Isle and at Lunna Taing. In addition, early ecclesiastical finds have been made on the tidal isle of Brough-of-Birsay. However, most of the hermit-settlements probably consisted of insubstantial wooden huts which have left no visible traces in the landscape.

Beyond Scotland, there are the indications that Irish eremetical settlement extended further north and west across the Atlantic – reaching the Faroe Islands and Iceland, at least by the eighth century. These migrations by Irish eremites provide the basis for the story of St. Brendan the Navigator. The cult of Brendan became established in the Faroes, where Brandansvick supposedly commemorates the place where he landed. Episodes in his Latin *Life*, which was probably written about 800 AD, and incidents in the more highly-embroidered 'Voyage of St. Brendan', have the saintly explorer and his companions sailing amongst 'columns of crystal' and islands from which fire

---

One day, a pillar in the sea appeared to them .... It had the colour of silver, but they thought that it seemed harder than marble. The pillar was of bright crystal.
One another day, there appeared to them ... a high mountain in the ocean .... It was very smoky on top .... When they looked back from a distance at the island, they saw that the mountain was ... spouting flames .... The whole mountain from the summit right down to the sea looked like one big pyre.

The Voyage of St. Brendan.

The island was stony and without grass .... the brothers began to carry the raw meat out of the boat ... which they had brought from the other island. When they had done this, they put a pot over a fire. When, however ... the pot began to boil, the 'island' began to be in motion like a wave. The brothers rushed to the boat, crying out for protection to the holy father .... He said to them: 'My sons, do not be afraid .... Where we were was not an island, but a fish – the foremost of all that swim in the ocean .... His name is Jasconius'.

The Voyage of St. Brendan, 18–19. The medieval voyage-tale is based on a 'Life' of St. Brendan, which was written probably around the end of the 8thc. The name 'Jasconius' may derive from the Irish *iasc*, a fish.

erupted. It seems clear that the authors were familiar with accounts of sea-journeys north of the Arctic Circle, which described icebergs and volcanoes.

An Irish scholar named Dícuil, an alumnus of Iona, compiled a geographical tract in the 820s which indicates an Irish presence in the 'Sheep Islands' (probably the Faroes) and implies settlement in Iceland before 790. The tract was written in France, where Dícuil was then living; he was probably amongst those who had left Iona after the devastating attack of 806, when the Columban community transferred its centre of administration to Kells (Co. Meath). Not surprisingly, he assumes that, by the time of writing, the Irish hermits further north had all abandoned their positions because of viking raids. Much later, Ari Fróði ('the learned') in his *Islendingabók* asserts that the *papar* fled on the arrival of the Vikings, leaving behind their 'bells, books and

There is another set of small islands, nearly all separated by narrow stretches of water; in these, for nearly a hundred years, hermits sailing from our country, Ireland, have lived. But just as they were always deserted from the beginning of the world, so now, because of the Northman pirates, they are emptied of anchorites, and filled with countless sheep and very many diverse kinds of sea-birds. I have never found these islands mentioned in the authorities.

Dícuil, *The Book of the Measurement of the Earth*, vii. Dícuil, an alumnus of Iona, writing in the 820s, discusses islands commonly identified with the Faroes; the Scandinavian *Faer-eyjar* means 'Sheep Islands'.

'The conversion of Iceland to Christianity, perhaps through some Irish influence, shown in this painting by Tom Lovell, marked the end of the great Viking era and the beginning of the Middle Ages.

croziers'. This is often quoted as meaning an 'immediate abandonment' of the Irish hermitages – but it is a 'traditional history' of Iceland, written some three hundred years after the events it purports to describe.

It is probable that the *popae* or *papar* maintained a presence in the North Atlantic into the 'Viking Age' – especially in the light of a traditional date in the second half of the ninth century for the arrival of the Scandinavians in Iceland. Significantly, the twelfth-century Icelandic *Landnámabók* ('Book of the Land-taking') claims that there were *papar* at Kirkjubaer ('Church Farm') when Ketill *inn fíflski* ('the foolish') brought his people to that district in the 870s. Unfortunately, archaeological evidence for Irish eremetical settlement in these parts remains elusive, although some maintain that field-systems of recognisably 'Celtic' type are to be found in the Faroe Islands. More persuasive testimony is offered by location-names which preserve the element *pap* in the Faroes and, even more to the point, in south-eastern Iceland. This area, for example, includes Papey and Papafjörður; even more notable is Pappyli – the dwelling of the *papar*. These suggest that at least a scattering of hermits remained in the country for some time, so that they and their settlements became known to the Scandinavian adventurers.

Some degree of overlap in time between eremetical settlement and Scandinavian colonisation should scarcely be surprising. Although the newcomers were (mostly) pagan, it did not follow that they were intent on eradicating every trace of Christianity they found; certainly, they tolerated ecclesiastical sites in the immediate hinterland of Dublin and other settlement areas in Ireland. Similarly, in Normandy they allowed churches and monasteries to continue. In all probability Christianity, and some of the ways of life associated with it, appeared strange to them, but they need not have felt threatened by it. Besides, although some doubtless aspired to the viking lifestyle, it is likely that most of those who undertook exploration of remote regions to find new areas for settlement were less interested in plunder; otherwise they would surely have directed their attentions towards populated areas. Nor is it necessary that all interaction between Norsemen and eremites was of a violent nature; indeed, there are good grounds for

---

It is now thirty years since clerics, who had lived on the island from the first of February to the first of August, told me that not only at the summer solstice, but in the days round about it, the sun setting in the evening hides itself as though behind a small hill in such a way that there was no darkness in that very small space of time, and a man could do whatever he wished as though the sun were there . . . . In the middle of that moment in time, it is midnight at the equator and thus, on the contrary, I think that at the winter solstice and for a few days about it dawn appears only for the smallest space at Thule, when it is noon at the equator.

Therefore, those authors are wrong . . . who have written that the sea will be solid about Thule, and that day without night continues right through from the vernal to the autumnal equinox, and that vice-versa night continues from the autumnal to the vernal equinox, since these men (Irish clerics) . . . had day and night alternately except for the period of the solstice. But one day's sail north of that they did find the sea frozen over.

Dícuil, *The Book of the Measurement of the Earth*, vii, paras 11–13. Dícuil discusses Thule – generally identified as Iceland.

> But before Iceland was settled from Norway, there were men there whom the Norse men style 'papar'. These were Christians, and people consider that they must have been from the British Isles, because there were found left behind them Irish books, bells and croziers, and other things besides, from which it might be deduced that they were Vestmenn, Irishmen.
>
> *Landnámabók* (Book of the Settlements), in Jones (ed.), *The Norse Atlantic Saga*, 112. © Oxford University Press 1964, 1986.

the proposition that the first Scandinavians to reach Iceland followed the maritime trail of Irish clerics from the Northern Isles of Scotland.

The Settlement of Iceland: Scandinavians and Irish?

The story of the early settlement of Iceland is told in twelfth and thirteenth century works of literature compiled long after Christianity – and literacy – had become established. Mention has already been made of Ari's *Islendingabók*, and of the *Landnámabók*, which supplies the fullest version of the story. Such accounts probably do preserve genuine memories of the colonial era, but by the time they were committed to writing, recollection would have been influenced by political developments of the intervening centuries. The tendency in such situations is to cast the narrative in a form that would make sense to (and gain the approval of) people of the writer's time.

The Scandinavian settlement of Iceland is commonly associated with the reign of the Norwegian king Haraldr *hárfagri*, and the story is that, as he extended his authority over various regions of southern Norway, some local rulers felt obliged to emigrate. That Haraldr was in some way linked with an emigration movement is not implausible – even if some of the early Norwegian settlers were most likely 'king's men' rather than opponents of royal authority. However, there are problems with the chronology of Haraldr and with the battle of Hafrsfjord, which seemingly gave him dominance of Rogaland; most historians are now inclined to date the battle, and the king's reign, to the closing years of the ninth century. In that event, his involvement need not have been with the earliest pioneering activities but with a 'second generation settlement'. Either way, Norwegian migration to Iceland – probably via the Faroe Islands – makes geographical sense, and close links between the two countries can be clearly seen in the subsequent historical record.

Medieval Icelandic accounts also highlight the contribution made to the early colony by another population-element, the Irish Norsemen. In view of the clear Norwegian connections of the Dublin settlers, and their close involvement with the Scottish Isles, such claims are not unreasonable. Besides, the early colonisation of Iceland broadly coincides with the so-called 'forty years rest' – an apparent fall-off in viking activity reflected in the Irish record for the later ninth century. Several pioneer figures of the Scandinavian North-Atlantic are given bynames which suggest close links with Ireland, or at least with a Gaelic-speaking milieu. According to tradition, the first settler in the Faroe Islands was Grim Kamban – which seems to represent the Irish sobriquet *Cammán*, a little stooped fellow. Icelandic sources assign prominent roles to a number of settlers with explicit Irish connections. For example, Audr (daughter of the Hebridean-based Ketill, who campaigned in Ireland), according to the Icelanders, was the wife of Ólafr, king of Dublin. Amongst others who were said to have come from Ireland were the brothers Ingólfr and Leif. The latter was called *Hjor*

The foster brothers Ingolf and Leif went on viking cruises . . . Leif went . . . harrying in Ireland . . . and from there on was known as Hjor-Leif, Sword-Leif. Hjorleif harried far and wide in Ireland, winning great riches there and taking captive ten thralls . . . .

Hjorleif stayed there (in Iceland) that winter; then in the spring . . . they set off to hunt . . . the thralls attacked each his appointed prey and murdered them to the last man.

Ingolf . . . went to look for the thralls, and found them in the islands . . . . Ingolf killed them all . . . . The islands where these thralls were killed have been known ever since as the Vestmannaeyjar, because they were Vestmenn, Irishmen.

Landnámabók (Book of the Settlements), in Jones (ed.), *The Norse Atlantic Saga*, 119, 120, 121. © Oxford University Press 1964, 1986.

Leif, from the sword which he allegedly took from an Irish burial mound. It is related that he had Irish servants, who rebelled and murdered him. Having sought refuge on the islands of Vestmannaeyjar, off the south coast of Iceland, they were hunted down and killed.

That Dublin-based Scandinavian adventurers should have had Irish servants is perfectly credible. Indeed it is possible, in view of Irish-Scandinavian military collaboration from the 850s onwards, that some viking warlords could have involved Irish retainers, or even allies, in their colonial endeavours. Almost certainly, the Vestmannaeyjar islands indicate the presence in Iceland of Irish settlers that were not hermits. The Scandinavians, as noted above, referred to themselves as *Østmen*, or 'Eastmen', and called the Irish 'Westmen'. There are, as it happens, some forty Irish placenames in Iceland, and a number of Irish words were borrowed into the Icelandic language, such as *kapall* (*capall* – a horse), *tarfur* (*tarb* – a bull) and *minntak* (*min* – grain). In addition, Iceland has an inheritance of Irish personal names such as Njal (Niall), Kormlud (Gormlaith), Kormakr (Cormac) and Finn (Find). The fact that over eighty individuals with Gaelic Irish names feature in Iceland's heroic literature, while episodes in surviving sagas point to the former existence of an epic ('Brian's Saga') revolving around Brian Bóruma, strongly suggests that there were close links between Ireland and Iceland at the highest social levels. Questions remain, however, regarding the scale of Irish involvement, and the period to which it may relate.

The medieval Icelandic accounts imply that native Irish nobility had a part in the colonisation of Iceland from the earliest stages. The *Landnámabók* catalogues over three hundred individuals among the most prominent early settlers. About 20% of these have Irish names or sobriquets, or are said to have come from Ireland. If this is accurate, it is curious that a recent study of burials from Iceland's 'Pre-Christian' period (i.e. before 1000 AD), focusing upon constellations of skeletal features (and not, it is emphasised, on 'biologically defined types'), notes a low degree of correspondence between Icelandic remains and samples from Ireland. Nonetheless, the *Landnámabók* claims that several of the original settlers belonged to the family of Cerball (d. 888), son of Dúngal, king of Osraige. Four daughters of Cerball were said to be wives of colonial magnates, while a son, grandson and other alleged male descendants of his are given major roles in the settlement process. However, the family relationships outlined in this account do not fit comfortably with surviving Irish genealogies. Similarly, hints from Icelandic tradition that Cerball exercised some form of lordship or protectorate over Dublin, and campaigned in the Hebrides, do not fit well with contemporary Irish sources.

Admittedly, a degree of historical haze surrounds the career of Cerball son of Dúngal. He belongs to a period (in the ninth century) when the rulers of Osraige were still establishing themselves as a political force in the Munster-Leinster marchlands. The fullest account of Cerball comes from a late source known as the *Fragmentary Annals of Ireland.* Even if this contains a genuine contemporary record, it has clearly been much embellished with later literary material, and a great deal of research needs to be done before its value can be fully appreciated. The exploits with which he is credited in Munster and Leinster are probably historical, and claims that he arrived at some compromise with the king of Tara, Máel-Sechnaill, may well be authentic. Beyond that, it is difficult to be certain. However, Cerball's personal achievement aside, his descendants certainly did assert a lordship over northern Leinster in the years after the Battle of Clontarf. Other dynasties from southern Ireland attained political supremacy of a still higher order. Diarmait mac Máele-na-mbó was successful in extending his authority not only over northern Leinster but over Dublin and, it appears, the Western Isles. Subsequently, the Ua Briain kings pursued political objectives in the Isle of Man and in the Hebrides and, although drawn into conflict with King Magnus of Norway, entered into a Scandinavian zone of which Iceland formed part. Presumably, this is the context for the composition of 'Brian's Saga', echoes of which can be found in surviving Icelandic medieval literature. In the light of these developments, there is probably a stronger case for viewing Irish dynastic connections with Iceland as a product not of early colonial links, but of eleventh or twelfth century alliances.

Modern Inuit, a descendant of those American natives who encountered the Vikings.

In summary, then, there is ample evidence to show that the north Atlantic route from Scotland, via the Faroes, to Iceland was first explored by Irish hermits. It seems reasonable to accept that the colonists followed the trail of hermit-settlers, and that there was some degree of overlap in the two phases of occupation. Undoubtedly, the colonisation of Iceland from the ninth century onwards was overwhelmingly Norwegian, although some Irish element is reflected in placenames, personal names and in later sources. Numbers of Irish were probably insignificant in the early colonial period (beyond a small number of servants), which perhaps explains the patterns of skeletal features in graves of pre-1000 AD. Such Irish presence as there was, especially at higher social levels, probably owed more to eleventh and twelfth-century developments. Of course, sources of the twelfth to thirteenth centuries (like the *Landnámabók*) claimed links with Irish royalty of the ninth century; but medieval Icelandic aristocrats probably wished to associate their Irish antecedents with the early days of the colony – in much the same way as certain modern New Englanders like to imagine that their ancestors arrived on the 'Mayflower'!

Explorations in the 'New World'

There would seem to be little basis for claims regarding an early Irish role in exploration further west, into what became the ultimate Scandinavian frontier. In the past, many have viewed the legend of St. Brendan as evidence for the discovery of America, if not by the saint himself, by Irish monks who later followed his trail. Granted, an episode in the 'Voyage of St. Brendan', in which a bird brings the monks a cluster of grapes, prompts questions in the light of later Icelandic accounts of the north American territory of *Vinland*. A version of the 'Life of St. Brendan' in the Book of Lismore relates an incident in which the monks encounter small dark men; some have been tempted to see in this a reference to North American peoples (whether Inuit or Amero-Indian), referred to in later Icelandic sources as 'Skraelings'. Aside from the fact that this particular episode belongs to a late version of the legend and could well be an addition, it must be borne in mind that the entire Brendan story is an allegory of the 'life pilgrimage' undertaken by ascetic clerics. Birds bearing grapes, or dark men, could merely be images of biblical inspiration representing, perhaps, divine assistance and forces of evil.

Icelandic accounts give tantalising hints of an Irish presence in the north-west Atlantic, but all of these episodes are frustratingly vague. They also feature in sources of twelfth or thirteenth century date, which makes it difficult to decide the period to which the stories might belong. The *Landnámabók* alludes to a land called 'Ireland the Great' which was said to lie 'west in the sea near Vinland the Good'; one saga describes how some adventurers met a group of Skraelings, who said that near their country there were white-robed men who 'marched in procession bearing poles before them'; another saga-fragment relates how a Norseman with a Dublin or Irish background, storm-driven onto a coast somewhere west of Iceland, was rescued by people who told him that he was 'in the White Man's land', in a language which, although not Scandinavian, he could recognise. Even if it is accepted that some territory near Vinland was discovered by

men with Irish connections, and that the above accounts describe a community of Christian clergy in Inuit territory, and an outlying colony which possibly spoke Irish (or an Irish dialect of Norse?), it is probable that these represent recollections of eleventh or twelfth-century experiences collected a hundred years or more later. In other words, they post-date the Christianisation of Iceland and the accelerated contact with Ireland that followed the assertion of Irish rule over Dublin and the Western Isles.

Greenland

One tradition ascribes the first sighting of Greenland to Norwegian navigator Gunnbjørn Ulf Krakason, who (again, perhaps reflecting later connections) is said to have sailed from Dublin around 930 AD. Not surprisingly, the medieval literature of Iceland emphasises the role of the late tenth-century Icelandic pioneer Erik the Red, and that of his sons, particularly Leif. The adventures of these explorers feature in the already-mentioned *Islendingabók*, but are recounted in great detail in the *Graenlendinga saga* (Saga of the Greenlanders) and *Eiríks saga rauða* (Saga of Erik the Red). From the turn of the tenth-eleventh centuries, settlers were drawn mainly to the southern and south-western coasts of Greenland, where the land had reasonably good agricultural potential. At the head of a fjord to which he gave his name, Erik established a farm which became known as Brattahlíð. Archaeological excavation has revealed traces of a house, a church and a burial ground at the site. Not far distant was another farming settlement at Garðar, while the principal colonies of Østerbygd (Eastern Settlement) and Vesterbygd (Western Settlement) were near to modern Julianehåb and Godthåb, respectively. Around the Amaralla Fjord, to the south of Vesterbygd, archaeologists have found traces of settlement dated by radiocarbon testing to (plus or minus) 1000 AD.

That same summer, a ship arrived in Greenland from Norway. Her captain was a man named Thorfinn Karlsefni [who] ... spent the winter at Brattahlid with Leif Eiriksson.

There was the same talk and to-do over the Vinland voyages as before, and the people there ... put strong pressure on Karlsefni to undertake an expedition. So his voyage was decided on, and he secured himself a ship's company of sixty men and five women .... They took with them all sorts of livestock, for it was their intention to colonise the country .... Karlsefni asked Leif for his house in Vinland. He would lend the house, he said, but not give it.

Next, then, they sailed their ship to sea and reached Leifsbudir all safe and sound, and carried their sleeping-bags ashore .... They took every advantage of the resources the country had to offer, both in the way of grapes and all kinds of hunting and fishing and good things.

Graenlendinga saga (Saga of the Greenlanders) in Jones (ed.), *The Norse Atlantic Saga*, 112. © Oxford University Press 1964, 1986.

The Greenland colonists of medieval times certainly engaged in agriculture, particularly stock-raising. Some, presumably the most prosperous, raised cattle, but the majority kept sheep and goats. They were also fishermen, hunters and trappers. Seal, walrus and reindeer were of prime economic importance; the skins of these animals and walrus ivory

Vikings in Vinland: the landing. Thorfinn Karlsefni and his party. Painting by Tom Lovell.

were their principal exports. This hunting-trapping economy is illustrated by finds from the Amaralla Fjord settlement. Development of the colony proceeded slowly. It was necessary to import timber (for all practical purposes unobtainable in Greenland) for construction and iron for fabrication of tools and weapons.

From about the year 1000 AD, further voyages of exploration to the west and south were undertaken by Leif Eriksson, his brothers Thorvald and Thorstein and a companion named Thorfinn Karlsefni. Their travels (allegedly undertaken at the urging of the Norwegian king, Ólafr Tryggvason, who died *c.*1000) brought them to new territories, to which the sagas give topographical names. These include *Helluland*, a district of rocky slabs which has been equated with Baffin Island; *Markland*, a forested region probably to be identified with the Labrador Coast; and *Vinland* – an area in which vines grew – thought to be around the Gulf of St. Lawrence. Much is made of the discovery of wild grapes, which apparently were regarded as something of a wonder. One is reminded of the episode in the 'Voyage of St. Brendan' in which a bird is said to have carried grapes to the Irish monks – even if this merely represented biblical imagery.

Several stories are related of encounters between the Icelanders and native peoples whom they called 'Skraelings'. Formerly, there was much debate as to whether these people were Inuit or Amero-Indian. The term, which means 'dark foreigners', was doubtless applied to peoples of different ethnic origin and should be interpreted in the light of where the episode concerned was located. The 'Skraelings' encountered by Thorvald Eriksson on the coast of *Markland*, if it may be identified with Labrador, were probably a people of Algonquian

> Karlsefni sailed south . . . into the estuary, and called the place Hop, Landlock Bay . . . .
>
> They were there for a fortnight . . . . Then early one morning . . . they saw nine skin-boats . . . and those others rowed towards them . . . They were small dark ill-favoured men, and had ugly hair on their heads. They had big eyes and were broad in the cheeks.
>
> Karlsefni and his men built themselves dwellings up above the lake . . . They now spent the winter there . . . But once spring came in they chanced early one morning to see how a multitude of skin-boats came rowing from the south . . . . Karlsefni and his men raised their shields, and they began trading together. Above all, these people wanted to buy red cloth. They also wanted to buy swords and spears, but this Karlsefni and Snorri would not allow. They had dark unblemished skins to exchange for the cloth and were taking a span's length of cloth for a skin, and this they tied round their heads.
>
> *Eiríks saga rauða*, in Jones (ed.), *The Norse Atlantic Saga*, 112. © Oxford University Press 1964, 1986.

stock. In other episodes, it seems more likely that Inuits or Inuks were intended. Be that as it may, the Greenlanders, having encountered people native to this forest region, became involved in a dispute which was apparently of their own making. In a resulting fracas, Thorvald and several of his party were killed.

According to the *Graenlendinga saga*, Thorfinn Karlsefni established a colony of 160 men and an unrecorded number of women in *Vinland*. They settled, with their livestock, and lived peaceably for some years; it is said that his son Snorri was born there. They traded with the 'Skraelings', but eventually disagreement arose and Thorfinn, realising that he could not hope to win a war against the native population, decided to abandon the settlement. Although the location of Thorfinn's colony is not recorded, it is tempting to identify it with the archaeological site of L'Anse aux Meadows, in northern Newfoundland. Certainly this site, excavated in the 1960s and 1970s, yielded the foundations of no fewer than eight Scandinavian-style houses, three of them multi-roomed halls. Even if no evidence of farming was found, there was abundant evidence of craftwork, including iron-working, boat repair and cloth production – which suggests the presence of women. Among the finds was a ringed pin of Irish type, which is interesting in the light of the Icelandic saga-fragments hinting at an Irish (or Hiberno-Norse?) presence in the 'New World'.

The scarcity of available evidence leaves us with many unanswered questions in relation to the Vinland venture. To date, L'Anse aux Meadows is the only North American location to produce conclusive evidence of medieval Norse settlement. Whether or not the colony expanded beyond that, or how long it survived, remains unknown. Curiously, an inscription at Hønen (in Ringerike), which has been dated to *c.*1050, commemorates the voyage of one Finn Fegin to Vinland. The implication of this is that the Norwegian homeland maintained close contacts not only with Iceland, but with the 'New World' colonies further west. The fact remains, however, that the Vinland colony was ultimately abandoned and even its location forgotten – although there are archaeological indicators of continued contact between the Greenlanders and the Inuk peoples, extending from Baffin Island into the High Arctic, which persisted into the thirteenth century and later.

Timeline: Settlers in the North Atlantic		
	Developments in North Atlantic	Developments in Ireland
750	Irish eremetical settlement in Faroes Irish eremetical settlement in Iceland	
800		Earliest Viking raids Latin 'Life' of St. Brendan Dícuil produces his geography
850	Grim Kamban settles in Faroes Earliest Scandinavian settlements in Iceland (860s/70s) Ketill *inn fiflski* settles at Kirk Jubaer Settlements in Iceland under King Haraldr *hárfagri* (890s?)	Cerball king of Osraige active against the Vikings So-called 'forty years rest' – later decades of 9thC
900		Viking rulers expelled from Dublin (902) 'Grandsons of Ívarr' regain Dublin (917)
950	Sighting of Greenland by Gunnbjørn Ulf Krakason, a Dublin Norwegian (*c*.930)	
	Settlements in Greenland; Erik the Red establishes Brattahlíð	Dublin brought under tribute by Máel-Sechnaill of Tara (989)
1000	Explorations in Vinland by Leif Eriksson Settlement at L'Anse aux Meadows	Dublin controlled by Brian Bóruma
1050	Voyage of Finn Fegin to Vinland?	Last independent king of Dublin expelled by Diarmait (1052)
1100	Ari *Fróði* produces *Islendingabók* Compilation of *Landnámabók*	Ua Briain kings assert lordship in Isle of man and Hebrides – conflict with Magnus of Norway Production of 'Brian's Saga'
1150		

5. Scandinavians Overseas: Soldiers and Settlers

The 'Call of the Sword'

The popular dictum relating to medieval peoples, that some fight, some labour and some pray, is as valid in its application to the Scandinavians as to others. However, their military role made the most lasting impact on the popular imagination, from the earliest viking raids to the 'Great Armies' that sacked Hamburg, Nantes and Paris in the 840s, overran much of England a generation later, and conquered Normandy in the 920s.

The archaeological record attests to the military aspect of Scandinavian society as transplanted to insular and Continental Europe. Burials and settlement sites alike, from Russia to France to Britain and Ireland, have their quota of martial artefacts. Finds of weaponry include swords, axeheads, spearheads and arrowheads. Shield 'bosses' are a common feature in overseas discoveries; the 'boss' is the iron dome at the centre of

---

They had on them ... many-coloured, well-fitting, handsome, well-shaped, well-adjusted, enfolding tunics, over comfortable long vests. They had with them also great warlike, bright, beautiful, variegated shields, with bosses of brass, and elegant chains of bronze ....

They had on them also, crested golden helmets, set with sparkling transparent brilliant gems and precious stones, on the heads of chiefs and royal knights. They had with them also, shining, powerful, strong, graceful, sharp, glaring, bright, broad, well-set *Lochlann* axes, in the hands of chiefs and leaders, and heroes, and brave knights, for cutting and maiming the close well-fastened coats of mail. They had with them steel, strong, piercing, graceful, ornamental, smooth, sharp-pointed, bright-sided, keen, clean, azure, glittering, flashing, brilliant, handsome, straight, well-tempered, quick, sharp swords, in the beautiful white hands of chiefs and royal knights, for hewing and for hacking, for maiming and mutilating skins and bodies and skulls.

A fanciful twelfth-century description of Scandinavian warriors at the Battle of Clontarf. *Cogadh Gáedhel re Gallaib*, 163.

the shield, the purpose of which was to provide added protection for the hand. The rest of the shield, generally made of wood or leather, has more often than not disintegrated. Helmets or chain-mail shirts are rarely found outside Scandinavia and the best-preserved examples come from graves in southern Norway. Nonetheless, it is clear that they were known in the colonies, as representations in art illustrate. A warrior depicted on a tenth-century cross at Middleton, Yorkshire, is wearing a pointed helmet. Warriors featured on Grim's Cross (Kirk Michael, Isle of Man) seem to be wearing helmets with face-guards, while the spearman on Joalf's Cross (also in the Isle of Man) may be wearing a 'byrnie', or leather jacket reinforced with iron rings.

Of course, not all Scandinavian military activity meant aggression directed from outside against settled populations. Once the vikings began to establish permanent bases in the areas they were drawn to, they involved themselves in territorial politics. This is well illustrated in Ireland where, from the mid-ninth century when viking activity was perhaps at its height, Scandinavian leaders formed alliances with local rulers. In the centuries that followed, as these 'foreign hostiles' developed an Hiberno-Norse identity, they increasingly fought in the armies of Irish kings. It is also important to stress that not all Scandinavians were fighting men – at least not as a chosen way of life. Nor do all finds of weapons imply military activity. While swords are commonly seen as 'offensive weapons', spears and arrows could equally be the equipment of a hunter. We have already seen how the Greenlander pioneers in Vinland chose to abandon their colony rather than die fighting. They were hunters and farmers, rather than viking warriors.

Harvesting the Land and Sea

Agriculture was important to the Scandinavian settlers in Europe. In some areas, placenames can be an indicator to agricultural activity. The suffixes -torp and -tot, found in a number of Normandy placenames (e.g. Routot, or Yvetot, both west of Rouen), presumably represent the Scandinavian -toft, a homestead. The element -by, common in England

Merchants from overseas: painting by Nikolai Roerich. Tretjakov Gallery, Moscow.

(e.g. Whitby, or Selby, both in Yorkshire), is generally taken to indicate an unenclosed farm-site. However, historical accounts tell us little about day-to-day concerns such as farming, focusing more on the dramatic and the extraordinary, and the archaeological record in relation to agriculture tends to be limited. The survival rate of organic materials is generally poor; besides, not enough work has yet been done on rural settlement in Scandinavian colonial regions.

Still, the assumption is that – like the Greenlanders – Scandinavian settlers elsewhere raised cattle, sheep and goats and that both dry-stock farming and dairying were practised. Several Norse rural sites in northern Scotland have produced finds of animal bone, including remains of cattle. In Ireland, there are indications that cattle, sheep and pigs were slaughtered at several locations, including Dublin and Wexford. Presumably they were raised in the rural hinterland of these urban settlements. Evidence for dairying is even harder to isolate; but there may be some significance in the fact that a harbour on the south-west coast of Ireland, where traces of Scandinavian rural settlement are to be found, is called Smerwick – *Smør-vík*, or 'butter-haven'. Domestic fowl, including hens, geese and ducks, were also kept. As a general rule, these were egg-producers, being killed for the table only when they had finished laying.

Colonial Scandinavian farmers also engaged in tillage. Cereal crops, including oats and barley, were grown in northern Scotland; Orkney, in particular, has produced evidence for the growing of flax. At one site in Orkney (on Birsay), the remains of a kiln have been found, while at another (Orphir) a horizontal mill has come to light. In Ireland, at Cherrywood, Co. Dublin, where there are two apparently ninth century phases of Scandinavian occupation, finds include a curious circular structure with a sunken interior, perhaps a grain store, and a kiln. These features, however, may predate the Viking-Age occupational phase. At other locations in Ireland, such as Wexford, there is evidence that de-husked oats and barley (presumably grown in the hinterland) were kiln-dried in the later Hiberno-Scandinavian period. Cereals were also grown around Dublin; two plough-socks have been found in the Wood Quay excavations, and a bakers' palette, which suggests that grain was milled. It seems likely that this was done in the surrounding countryside, as there is little to show that milling was carried on in the town before *c*.1100 AD.

In earlier phases of settlement, fishing was probably conducted as a part-time activity to supplement the meagre incomes of smaller farms. The placenames Laxey (*Laks-ey*; 'salmon-isle') in the Isle of Man and Leixlip (*Laks-laup*; 'salmon-leap') on the Liffey, near Dublin, suggest the importance of salmon – even if the dating is uncertain. Although the Wood Quay site in Dublin has produced middens (refuse mounds) of oyster shells, some of which may be as early as the tenth century, most of the available material evidence belongs to the Late Norse and Medieval periods. Middens of Late Norse date in Shetland and in Caithness, Scotland, have yielded large quantities of fish bones, especially cod and ling. Similarly, a range of fish-remains – including

(top) Overhead view of Temple Bar excavation.

(right) Spearheads, harpoons, needle, and fishhooks, from Temple Bar.

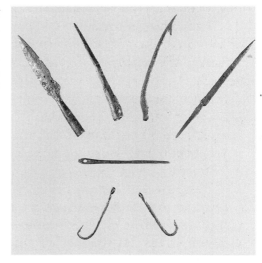

cod and ling, but also hake, whiting and herring – has come to light in Wexford mainly from thirteenth-century contexts. Perhaps by this time, the well-known lucrative export trade in dried fish had already developed. It appears that settlers of Scandinavian descent, even as the Viking Age slipped into history, still practised seal-hunting. From the historical record, we learn that ninth century vikings hunted seals (and, perhaps, porpoises) on Irish coasts. Archaeological remains show that seals were still being eaten, at least occasionally, in thirteenth-century Wexford.

Craftsmen and Traders

As Dublin developed as an urban centre, from about the mid-tenth century, its range of industry expanded. Aside from mineral-based industries like metalwork and jewellery, various crafts are represented which utilised organic materials – including wood, bone, leather and textiles. The archaeological value of Dublin in this regard owes much to the waterlogging of sites, ensuring the survival of organic matter which in other conditions would have disintegrated. Of the mineral-based industries, the most notable was almost certainly blacksmithing. The importance of blacksmiths to the economy was mainly due to the wide range of products which they manufactured. They are commonly thought of in connection with horseshoes, but in fact they fabricated chains and locks, hinges and hooks, staples, nails, and various weapons and tools. In Dublin, blacksmiths were mostly to be found outside the area of urban settlement, presumably because of smoke and smell, and the danger of fire; a similar trend can be noted in Waterford, where finds of slag (which indicate iron working) occur some distance south of the High Street.

There was, in fact, a general tendency for crafts to be concentrated in certain areas. The non-ferrous metalworkers of Dublin were grouped around Christchurch Place, where bronzesmiths, gold and silversmiths plied their trade. Mostly, they manufactured items of jewellery, including brooches, armlets and finger rings. They made extensive use of imported silver, many of their rings and bracelets being made of plaited

(top) Stone weights for various purposes, from Temple Bar dig.

(right) Carved button from Temple Bar dig.

(bottom) Turned wooden playing piece for a board game.

silver wire. In considering a medieval economy with relatively advanced metal technology, there is a danger that the importance of stonecutting as a craft might not be fully appreciated. The cutting of gritstone to make rotary querns for grinding corn (not to mention millstones) remained as important as ever. In addition, artificers utilised the relatively soft 'soapstone' for making bowls and lamps; they also fashioned a range of other stone implements, including sharpening stones, spindle whorls, loomweights and fishing weights. Specialist craftsmen shaped semi-precious stones for personal adornment, working amber, jet, cornelian and even glass to make pendants and beads. Because these semi-precious stones were not native to Ireland, it is tempting to suggest that they were imported not as rough stone but as finished products. However, flakes of amber and unworked lumps have come to light, which shows that working was carried out in Dublin.

The most important industry utilising organic material was undoubtedly woodwork. Carpenters were largely concerned with the production of planks and beams for house-building – but they also made furniture, as parts of chairs and benches have been found in the Dublin excavations. Woodcarvers fashioned smaller articles; containers, including jewellery boxes, and implements such as spoons, ladles, and game-pegs. A wider range of containers was supplied by the coopers, who bound together staves to form barrels, tubs, buckets and even mugs. Their craft was much in demand, as there was little local tradition of pottery-manufacture. Woodturners, working with pole-lathes, made various utensils such as bowls and platters, while basketmaking was also carried on.

Another craft which certainly involved wood was shipbuilding which, indeed, many would see as an industry in its own right. Indications that ships were at least repaired, if not built, in Dublin are provided by finds of ships' timbers reused in house-building. At Fishamble Street, part of a prow of ninth-century date found a new role as a threshold; at Winetavern Street, an eleventh-century ship-timber became a drain-cover. Perhaps of greater interest is the discovery in Denmark of a large eleventh-century ship (now in the Viking Ship Museum, Roskilde) built of Irish oak.

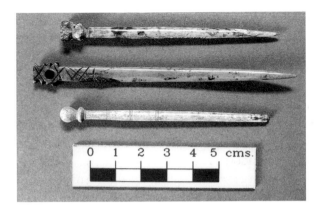

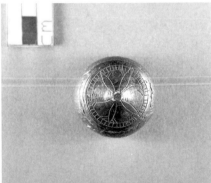

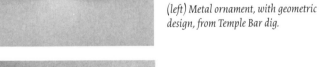

(top) Three bone pins, from Temple Bar, 1 July 1998.

(left) Metal ornament, with geometric design, from Temple Bar dig.

(bottom) Wooden ring, with incised carving.

Boneworkers, centred around Dublin's High Street, carved combs, pins and needles from bone, cattle-horn and red deer antler. Some pins were quite elaborate, decorated with animal heads. These craftsmen also produced gaming pieces, as did their counterparts in Wexford. Leatherworkers were also represented, although much of the evidence for their craft is indirect, in the form of tools. Finds include awls, needles, punches and at least one shoe-last – although fragments of shoes, scabbards and bags or satchels made of leather have come to light. Similarly, much of what is known of the activities of textileworkers is inferred from indirect evidence. Shears indicate the fleecing of sheep, spindle whorls point to spinning, while stone cylinders (presumably loom weights), weaving tablets (mostly of antler or bone) and a carved wooden weaving-sword handle (decorated with interlace design) all point to cloth-making. The work of embroidresses is represented by a selection of needles of bone or copper alloy. Some fragmentary remains of textiles illustrate the range of materials produced, from finely woven wool or linen to coarse sacking. Fabrics from abroad, including silk, were used in making dress items for the wealthy.

However, not all Hiberno-Scandinavian business activity was concerned with manufacturing. Trade and commerce were also important, and played no small part in generating the wealth which the Irish tract *Cogadh Gáedhel re Gallaib* attributed to Dublin and to Limerick. At least by the eleventh century, Dublin had its 'Merchants' Quay', and archaeological finds have included copper pans from balance-scales, of a type well known in Scandinavia, and sets of lead weights. The very uniformity of these weights suggests that some authority – royal or civic – had imposed a standard system of measures.

It may be assumed that agricultural produce was sold in the town, along with fish. Fishamble Street preserves reference to the market at which seafood was traded. This steep, narrow thoroughfare leads up from a point on the bank of the River Liffey known in medieval times as the 'Fyssche Slyppe'. While Ireland as a whole continued to operate a barter economy, Dublin was using coinage at least by the tenth century. Various Anglo-Saxon and foreign coins were used but, from the 990s,

Reconstruction from archaeological evidence of a house in Norse age Fishamble Street. National Museum of Ireland

King Sitriuc Silkenbeard began to issue his own coins based on Anglo-Saxon models. By this time, the operation of a mint had become, in England and elsewhere, a widely accepted status-indicator for towns.

Aside from internal trading, Dublin's business community engaged in intensive importing and exporting operations. While some raw materials, such as wood and antler, could be drawn from the hinterland, others had to be sourced from further afield. Like many Norse coastal settlements, Dublin was a busy port, which had direct contact with the Scandinavian homeland, with Britain and northern France, and oblique links with more distant lands. Many of the special varieties of stone used in carving and in jewellery manufacture were foreign, some coming from regions with which the Hiberno-Norsemen probably did not have direct dealings. Although soapstone was imported from the Northern Isles of Scotland and jet apparently from York, amber is invariably associated with the Baltic and cornelian with Central Europe. Metals which are understood to be non-native include tin, assumed to be from Cornwall, and silver, believed to have originated in the Arab world. Other raw materials from abroad included furs and walrus ivory from the Arctic lands, and silk which came ultimately from the Byzantine Empire. The aristocracy demanded additional luxury items, such as ponies from Wales and wine from France, while at least some manufactured goods were imported, including pottery from Chester and high-class weapons. Swords were, of course, fabricated in Dublin, but some Frankish and Anglo-Saxon specimens have been found – presumably ordered in by fashion-conscious gentry.

Exports from the Hiberno-Norse ports are less evident. However, from its beginnings, Dublin had dealt in slaves, and it is probable that at least some of these were traded abroad. Cattle hides were an established Irish export, and it appears that the Scandinavians continued this tradition; there is an account from the Viking Age of a ship carrying hides to Poitou, in Western France. Timber was another traditional export and, as remarked above, a ship found near Roskilde, Denmark, was built of Irish oak. Questions could validly be raised as to whether this particular vessel was built in Denmark from Irish timber, or was built in Ireland for export. In any event, it is very possible that Dublin, and perhaps other Hiberno-Norse ports, repaired and provisioned ships en route from one part of the Scandinavian world to another.

Evidence for the export of manufactured goods by the Hiberno-Norsemen is scarce, but arm-rings of Irish-Scandinavian origin have been found in Norwegian hoards, notably at Bostrand and Grimestad.

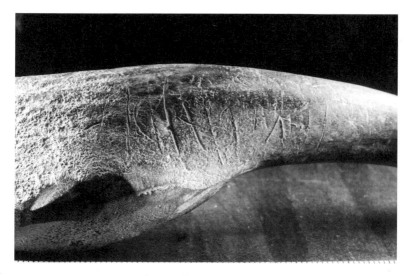

Trial piece with incised runic lettering.

Similarly, Irish ringed pins (a form of cloak-pin) were bartered overseas, and some of these went to Iceland. At least one specimen was found at the Greenlander colonial site of L'Anse aux Meadows, Newfoundland; this, at the very least, highlights the need to search for further material evidence of Irish connections with that region.

Role of Christianity

The Norse colonists were apparently tolerant of Christian ecclesiastical foundations in the hinterland of their settlements, even in the early stages when it might be assumed that the incomers were heathen. Dublin, like the other principal Norse settlements in Ireland, was surrounded by ecclesiastical sites which continued as the record shows, to flourish through the ninth and tenth centuries. A similar trend can be observed in relation to Rouen, Normandy, where tenth-century Norse colonists under Rollo appear not to have disturbed surrounding church foundations. Even the archbishop of Rouen remained in office. There may well have been an element of self-interest in this 'open-

(right) Skate with incised decoration.

(bottom) Bone pin with incised decoration.

mindedness', with taxes, perhaps in the form of food and other supplies, being levied on the ecclesiastical estates. However, it is clear that from about the middle of the tenth century the Hiberno-Norsemen were not only adopting Christianity but were practising devotion to 'saints of the Irish tradition'. The Dubliners, in particular, adopted the cult of St. Columba of Iona, along with that of St. Patrick.

As in Normandy, where Rollo and more particularly his son William Longsword proceeded to endow churches, the Norse of Ireland were founding churches of their own, certainly from the early eleventh century. Around 1028, King Sitriuc Silkenbeard established an episcopal see at Dublin and founded the cathedral church of the Holy Trinity (later known as Christ Church). The decades that followed saw the establishment of churches for parish communities; one of the earliest was dedicated to St. Olave, the Norwegian king Ólafr Haraldson, who played a major part in promoting Christianity in Norway and who was killed in 1030. It may be significant that one of the oldest pre-conquest churches in York likewise commemorated St. Olave. By the twelfth century, Dublin

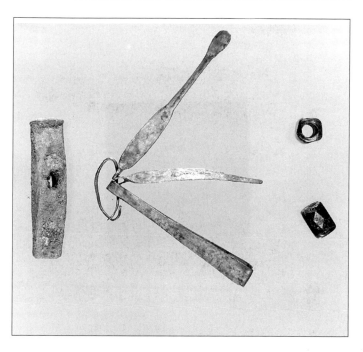

(top) Metal worker's hammer head (left), tweezers, scoop or measuring spoon, and blade (centre), semiprecious stones cut as ornaments, from Temple Bar dig.

(left) Stone mould for metal ingots.

had a network of parishes, mostly dedicated to Irish saints. Several were located on the southern fringes of the town, including the churches of St. Patrick (Patrick Street), St. Brigit (Bride Street), and St Kevin (Kevin Street). North of the Liffey, in the suburb of Oxmantown (Østmanby, Østmantun), was the church of St. Michan – seemingly dedicated to St. Cainnech, also known as Mo-Chainne. Twelfth-century Waterford, also a bishop's see, had at least two parish churches; one was dedicated to St. Olave, the other to St. Peter.

The gradual penetration of Christianity into the Scandinavian world owed much to German missionary effort, and to English and Irish connections. Although some Danish kings were baptised as early as the mid-ninth century, and missionary activity began to spread northwards from Hamburg-Bremen, the conversion of the Scandinavian peoples proceeded slowly. By the mid-tenth century, missionary bishoprics were established in Jutland, and the reign of King Harald Bluetooth (d. 987) is associated with the establishment on a sound footing of the Christian faith in Denmark. He founded a church at Jelling, on the site of an Iron Age complex. Harald's dynasty was closely associated with York and, indeed, pursued political ambitions in England with considerable success. A contemporary Norwegian king, Hákon (d. 960), a foster-son of the English king Athelstan, was reared as a Christian. However, although he introduced clergy to the country and founded churches, he does not appear to have directly confronted pagan institutions.

Of his successors, Ólafr Tryggvason (d. 1000) and Ólafr Haraldson (d. 1030) are best remembered for active promotion of Christianity in Norway, although they pursued this end often through forceful means and along with efforts to unite the country under a single rule. The short reign of Ólafr Tryggvason saw two significant enshrinements – the bones of the holy men of Selja, and the body of St. Sunniva. The origins of the latter are shrouded in obscurity. Her name appears to be Anglo-Saxon, but the fact that Norwegian tradition represents her as Irish suggests a consciousness of some link between Ireland and the introduction of the faith. It is probably significant that a version of the 'Voyage of St. Brendan' was translated into Old Norse. As for King Ólafr Haraldson, his fifteen-year

(top) Viking traders with Persian merchants on Russian riverbank. Painting by Tom Lovell.

(below left) The Christian king Olaf Tryggvason overthrowing the images of Thor the other Norse gods in the temple at Trondheim. Modern drawing from The Saga of Olaf Tryggvason *(London, 1911)*

(below right) Borgund, Norway, Stave church of 12th century, typical of churches in Viking lands after the conversion to Christianity.

reign ended with a battle against nobles who opposed his centralising policies and his enforced Christianisation; nonetheless, he was venerated as a saint.

> Now Olaf, placing all his trust in God, a second time resumed his war for the suppression of idolatry . . . .
>
> The most Christian king, noted for his firmness towards his enemies and justice toward his own people, believed that God had restored him to his kingdom in order that henceforth no one should be spared who either would persist in sorcery or would not become a Christian. He had for the most part made good his resolution when a small number of the sorcerers, who had survived, struck him down . . . .
>
> Thus Olaf, king and, as we believe, martyr, came to such an end. His body was entombed with becoming honour in the great city of his realm, Trondhjem . . . .
>
> The feast of his passion, observed on the fourth kalends of August, is worthily recalled with eternal veneration on the part of all the peoples of the Northern Ocean, the Norwegians, Swedes, Goths, Sembi, Danes and Slavs.
>
> Adam of Bremen, *History of the Archbishops of Hamburg-Bremen*, 96–7.

Meanwhile, in Sweden, German evangelists had succeeded in establishing a missionary bishopric in Våstergötland by the early eleventh century. This took place probably in the reign of Olofr Skötkonung (d. 1020), king of the Svear and the Götar, the first Swedish ruler known to have been a Christian. Nonetheless, widespread abandonment of old ways came only in the reign of his son, Anund Jakob (d. 1050). The eleventh century saw Christianity gain widespread acceptance in Sweden, as cross-inscribed runestones indicate. From that time on, the faith gradually made its way into the Swedish colonies in Russia.

The situation in Iceland is less clear-cut. In the light of close Irish connections, it is possible that some Christian influences were present in the early colony. Mention has already been made of Ketill *inn fiflski* and of the queen-consort Audr, both of whom are believed to have been Christian. A son (or descendant?) of Audr, named Orlygr, is credited with having built at Esjuberg, near Reykjavík, a church dedicated to St. Columba. However, even if these traditions are accepted, the numerical superiority of Norwegian settlers was undoubtedly enough to ensure that pagan belief and practice remained dominant throughout the tenth century. Later, the Norwegian king Ólafr Tryggvason (died *c.*1000) was credited with having compelled the Icelandic *Althing* (assembly) to formally adopt the Christian faith. The first bishop for Iceland was consecrated in 1056, but almost forty years elapsed before a permanent episcopal see was established at Skálholt. By this time, Christianity had taken firm root in the Faroe Islands – a development associated in tradition with a certain Sigmund Brestisson.

It was also learnt that there had been a change of religion in Norway. The old faith had been discarded, and King Olaf had also converted to Christianity the western lands – Shetland, Orkney and the Faroe Islands. Njal heard many people say that it was monstrous to forsake the old beliefs. But Njal replied 'In my opinion the new faith is much better; happy the man who receives it. And if the men who spread this faith come out to Iceland, I shall do all I can to further it'.

At the *Althing* that summer … the Christians tented their booths …. Next day both sides went to the Law Rock and both of them, Christians and heathens, named witnesses and renounced their community of laws.
The Christians … went to see Thorgeir the priest of Ljosawater and gave him three marks of silver to proclaim what the law should be ….
'The first principle of our laws' declared Thorgeir, 'is that all men in this land shall be Christian and believe in the one God – Father, Son and Holy Ghost – and renounce all worship of idols ….'
After that, the people went home from the *Althing*.

The conversion of Iceland to Christianity. *Njal's Saga*, 225–6.
Reproduced by permission of Penguin Books Ltd.

The settlements in Greenland, if they were not Christian from the beginning, adopted the faith at an early stage – perhaps even in the time of Erik the Red, or in that of his sons. At Brattahlíð, where Erik's family settled, archaeologists have excavated the site of a small turf-walled oratory with interior dimensions of only 3.5m x 2m. This appears to be the earliest church in Greenland. In the 1120s, Bishop

Erik Gnupsson established his see at Garðar. Although Greenlander efforts at colonisation in Newfoundland or on the Labrador coast had long been abandoned, Bishop Erik followed surviving trade routes to the Arctic lands of the Inuk peoples in an attempt to spread the faith in the 'New World'. However, he was soon recalled by his superiors in Norway, who perhaps considered that the frontiers of Christianity had already been advanced to limits beyond which a church community would not be viable. For centuries to come, the 'New World' would remain a realm of 'old faiths'.

Timeline: Soldiers and Settlers	
Developments in Continental Europe	Developments in Ireland
750	
Earliest Viking raids	Earliest Viking raids
800	
	Permanent settlement – Dublin as trading emporium
Great armies sack Hamburg, Nantes, Paris	
850	Military alliances between Vikings and Irish.
Great armies active in England	
	So-called 'forty years rest' – later decades of 9thC
900	
Settlements in Normandy	Re-establishment of Dublin (917)
950	Dublin develops as craft-centre.
Christianity established in Denmark	
	Waterford and Limerick emerge as commercial centres
1000 Christianity becomes established in Sweden, Norway and Iceland	
	Wexford emerges as a commercial centre
	Cathedral in Dublin (1028)
Christianity reaches Scandinavian colonies in Russia and Greenland	
1050	Last independent king of Dublin expelled by Diarmait (1052)
	Ship-building flourishes in Dublin
	Episcopal sees in Waterford, Limerick
1100	Parish churches established in Hiberno-Norse colonies
Episcopal see in Greenland	

The Vikings – Agents for Change?

Both the immediate impact of the vikings and their longer term influence in areas of colonial settlement have prompted much debate among historians. In Ireland, few scholars doubt that society in general, and the Christian church in particular, was shocked by the ninth-century viking raids. Not many, however, would now accept without reserve an argument that was strongly upheld in the 1960s, that the 'Viking Age' had dire long-term consequences both for the church and for socio-political organisation in Ireland. It was suggested that the upheaval brought about by these attacks was responsible for a general decline in moral standards whereby the 'monastic fervour' of Early Christian Ireland dissipated, leaving the church secularised and politicised.

Perhaps, over time, the medieval Irish church did develop a number of curious organisational traits, some of which were viewed by commentators (medieval and modern) as abuses. It became common for abbots to be laymen (or men in minor orders only), while married clergy often made ecclesiastical offices and properties into hereditary possessions. Such closed family interests in turn promoted politicisation and caused church settlements to become embroiled in warfare. Political organisation in Ireland was also subject to gradual change; there seems to have been a greater level of militarisation, while kingship became more tightly concentrated as a smaller number of ambitious dynasties increased their power. Little by little, the status of petty kings was eroded with the emergence of stronger overkingships.

Social and political change of this order certainly took place in medieval Ireland. The issue for debate relates to the timespan over which such developments took place, and the likely impact of the 'Viking Age' as a catalyst for change. Did the vikings cause such consternation amongst the Irish that they induced the 'passing of the Old Order'? An alternative view, rooted more firmly in a closer scrutiny of the annals, places the developments in question in a longer perspective. Several of the trends, both in the church and in kingship, can be seen to pre-date the vikings, while others display a complex inter-relationship over a longer period of time. It is probable, therefore, that the impact of the vikings as a factor in socio-political change may have been exaggerated in the past. At the same time, wherever they settled (and Ireland was no exception) the Scandinavians left their mark in various socio-economic spheres. They made a significant contribution to the development of military and maritime technology, trade and commerce, language and naming-practices, settlement patterns, and art and literature.

Scandinavian Influence and Cultural Exchange

The military and naval influence of the Norsemen was considerable in terms of range and geographical extent. In Ireland, from as early as the mid-ninth century, viking bands were joining forces with native rulers. In the tenth century, as Hiberno-Scandinavian kingships gradually integrated into the Irish pattern, the formation of political and military alliances accelerated. Given their continued involvement in political struggles over several centuries, it should scarcely surprise us that the Norsemen, aside from being active participants, contributed significantly to the development of Irish warfare.

> They use, however, three types of weapons – short spears, two darts ... and big axes well and carefully forged, which they have taken over from the Norwegians and the Ostmen ....
>
> From an old and evil custom they always carry an axe in their hand as if it were a staff. In this way, if they have a feeling for any evil, they can the more quickly give it effect. Wherever they go they drag this along with them. When they see the opportunity, and the occasion presents itself, this weapon has not to be unsheathed as a sword, or bent as a bow, or poised as a spear. Without further preparation, beyond being raised a little, it inflicts a mortal blow. At hand, or rather in the hand, it is enough to cause death ....
>
> An account of the 'Irish axe'; Gerald of Wales, *The History and Topography of Ireland* (12th c.). Reproduced by permission of Penguin Books Ltd.

(top) Viking spear and axe head with wooden handle, found in the Shannon, a main raiding route of the Vikings into the heart of Ireland.

(bottom) Iron axehead, from Dublin. The Viking settlers introduced the use of axes into Ireland.

The Ballinderry game board, made of yew, found in an Irish context but the interlace decoration is of Scandinavian style.

At the most basic level their weaponry, the superior quality of which was recognised at an early stage, was widely copied. There is a general tendency, from the tenth century onwards, for Irish swords to be made longer and of higher grade iron, in imitation of Viking types – although the bow-and-arrow and chainmail coat were apparently not adopted until later medieval times. Meanwhile, however, usage of the Norse battle-axe was embraced with enthusiasm and became so common that, by the twelfth century, this weapon was regarded by foreign commentators as 'typically Irish'. Styles of warfare also changed. While naval fleets had a role in pre-Viking conflicts, the annal-record suggests that ships were used more widely from the tenth or eleventh centuries onwards, and that river fleets became a common feature in connection with inland campaigns. Brian Boruma used Hiberno-Scandinavian fleets to effect, as did his descendants the Ua Briain overkings of Munster, in their struggles for high-kingship of Ireland with the powerful rulers of Connacht and of

Carved whalebone plaque from Winetavern St. excavations.

the north. Some historians consider that an increased emphasis on cavalry was yet another outcome of conflict with the vikings, as their pattern of lightning raids made the rapid mobility of troops essential.

Scandinavian influence in seafaring, however, went beyond the adoption of naval strategies. Many new techniques of shipbuilding and seamanship were learned, and this is reflected in the Irish language, with various words relating to ships and to maritime activities, including fishing, borrowed from Old Norse. Included here are terms such as *bád* (ON *bátr*, a boat), *accaire* (ON *akkeri*, an anchor), *stiúir* (ON *styri*, a helm), while *scadán* (a herring) may be based on Old Norse. Of course the Irish had boats and sailors long before the arrival of the vikings, and presumably they also fished for herrings; however, the newcomers were so closely associated with these activities that their vocabulary was adopted more or less as a package and completely supplanted native terminology.

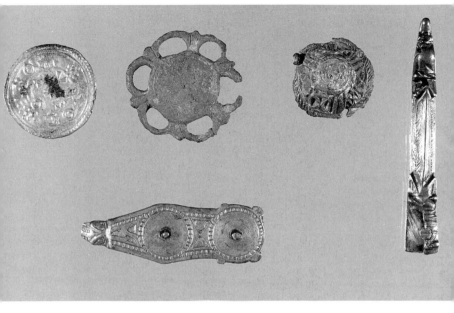

Gold and silver ornaments from Temple Bar dig.

While it is true that Ireland's economy was at a pre-monetary stage, trade undoubtedly flourished in pre-viking times. It is clear from native sources that there was a merchant class and that (at least from the Early Christian period, if not earlier) they had a system of weights and measures. Nonetheless, the Scandinavians – who created extensive overseas trade networks – introduced coinage to Ireland, and were perhaps responsible for new measurement standards. A range of Irish terms for money and for commercial activites, although their roots lay in other languages, were probably borrowed through Old Norse. Examples include *pingin* (Anglo-Saxon *penning*, a penny), *margad* (Latin *mercatura*, trade, market), and *mangaire* (Latin *mango*, to deal – hence a dealer). Nor was language-borrowing in one direction only. Terms relating to agriculture – in particular certain words for animals – were borrowed from Irish into Old Norse. Naming practice was another area in which

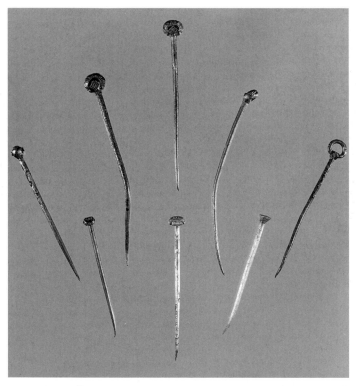

Eight clothing pins for personal use, from Temple Bar dig.

exchange took place. Not only did the Scandinavians adopt Gaelic names such as Niall and Cormac, but certain Old Norse appellations came into use amongst the Irish. Indeed, the adoption of such names as Amlaoib (Ólafr), Sitriuc (Sigtrygg) and later Magnus gave rise to surnames like Mac Amhlaoibh (McAuliffe), Mac Shitric (McKitterick) and Mac Maghnusa (McManus).

Another manifestation of Norse and Irish cultural exchange is the emergence of urban settlement. It was once held that 'the vikings' were responsible for founding 'cities' in Ireland; however, recent reassessment has shown that this is an oversimplified and misleading picture. The

The bookshrine of the Cathach, which features an Irish adoption of Ringereike ornament.

Scandinavian homeland of the viking period did not have cities. Certainly, settlements like Hedeby in Denmark, Kaupang in Norway or Birka in Sweden emerged as centres of craft-industry and trade, but it is now widely acknowledged that these sites lacked many of the criteria associated with genuine urban character. The same is true of Dublin.

The ninth-century settlement at the Liffey estuary might reasonably be described as a trading emporium, but hardly as a town, much less a city. Dublin's acquisition of an urban character was not clear until the later tenth/early eleventh century, by which time its inhabitants were no longer 'vikings' in the strict sense. More to the point, while the transition owed much to the initiative of York-based rulers, Irish influences can be clearly observed, especially in the evolution of house types. It is also significant that urban development at other locations in Ireland, including Limerick and Waterford, can be traced only from the end of the tenth century (at the earliest) and so comes after the assertion of Irish rule over the settlements in question. For this reason, it is probably more

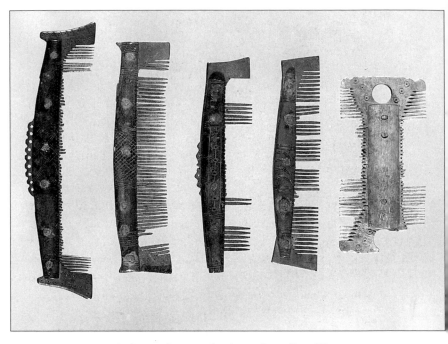

Five bone combs excavated at the Temple Bar dig, Dublin.

accurate to view the emergence of 'towns' in Ireland as a joint Irish-Scandinavian achievement.

Such cultural interface, especially from the tenth century onwards, also facilitated cross-influences in the arts. Styles of decoration were exchanged, so that Irish-type penannular ('almost ring-shaped') brooches, such as that found at Orton Scar, Cumbria, were produced by Scandinavian silversmiths. From the eleventh century onwards, Scandinavian art styles were adopted by Irish craftsmen. The Ringerike style, named from an area near Oslo and characterised by animal motifs with foliage tendrils, first made an impact in England and was already out-dated when it reached Ireland. However, Irish artists further developed the style, producing distinctive variations. A case in point is the 'Shrine of the Cathach', a copper-alloy plated box, embellished with silver

The shrine of St. Patrick's bell, a prime example of the widely spread Urnes style of decoration.

Pray for Cathbarr Ua Domnaill who caused this shrine to be made; for Sitriuc grandson of Áed who fashioned it, and for Domnall son of Robartach superior of Kells who [also] caused it to be made.

Inscription on the Shrine of 'The Cathach' dating to the late 11th century. (Translation by the author, 89.)

foil, made for an early psalter (psalm book) which was believed to have been transcribed by St. Columba himself. The box-shrine, with its Hiberno-Ringerike decoration, was jointly commissioned, according to an inscription, by Domnall son of Robartach, abbot of Kells, and Cathbarr Ua Domnaill, local ruler of Cenél Lugdach (a territory in Co. Donegal). It is mentioned in the annals under the year 1090.

An even later example of Hiberno-Ringerike art is a Gospel book produced in east Ulster – possibly in Bangor – seemingly in the 1120s. The decorated capital letters are formed as beasts in an interlace of foliage. The later Urnes style, so-called from the distinctive wood carvings on a church in western Norway, features patterns (often asymmetric) of slim biting animals and snakes interlaced with tendrils. An Irish version of this style appears on the early-twelfth century 'Shrine of St. Patrick's Bell', made for Domnall MacLochlainn (d. 1121), king of Cenél nÉogain, and Domnall (d. 1105) son of Amalgaid, abbot of Armagh.

Even before this, exchange of ideas in relation to literature had already taken place. By the time Amlaíb Cuarán (d. 981), king of Dublin, was commissioning Irish praise-poems, heroic poetry that had much in common with Germanic styles was already being written down in the Scandinavian homelands – much of it inscribed on runestones. The

Tales of the Fianna and their exploits in hunting and fighting reflect the Norse influence on Irish literature. Drawing by Patrick O'Byrne, 1919.

Magnus the Great came ashore fiercely with barbarous blade;
he burned from heather to sea of that part of Ireland he came upon.
With his right hand Magnus sought
battle with two thousand men on the beach
and challenged that with his left hand he would fight with the High King.
Comes news to the Fianna of destiny
that Magnus has arrived in their midst
and that he would not yield without a hard battle
with the Fianna of Ireland.

The Battle of Magnus, son of the king of Norway. Translation by the author.
Ó Siochfhradha (ed.), *Laoithe na Féinne*.

development of the saga as a literary genre, however, came late – from the eleventh or twelfth century onwards – and is particularly associated with Iceland. The evolution of this genre against a background of Irish lordship over Dublin and the Western Isles, and the consolidation of Irish-Icelandic links, is surely significant – especially as one of the early sagas celebrated Brian Bóruma. By this time, however, the descendants of Ireland's Scandinavian colonists were no longer described in Irish sources as *geinte* ('heathens'), or even *Lochlannaigh* ('Northmen') but, at least on occasion, as *Gaill Éirenn* ('the foreigners of Ireland') – as if to acknowledge, however reservedly, their right to be there. Already, by the twelfth century, an emerging cycle of heroic folk-literature, centred on Finn mac Cumaill and the Fianna warriors, could look back to a distant past when vikings, as giants from remote northern lands, engaged in contests with the legendary Finn.

Timeline: Scandinavian Heritage

	Political and economic developments in Ireland	Military and cultural developments in Ireland
750		
	Earliest Viking raids	
800		
	Permanent settlement – Dublin as trading emporium	
850		
	Military alliances between Vikings and Irish	
	So-called 'forty years rest' – later decades of 9thC	Increasing mention of fleets in Irish warfare
900		
	Re-establishment of Dublin (917)	Maritime and commercial terms borrowed into Irish from Old Norse
950	Dublin develops as craft-centre	
	Waterford and Limerick emerge as commercial centres	
1000	Wexford emerges as a commercial centre	
1050	Last independent king of Dublin expelled by Diarmait (1052)	
	Ship-building flourishes in Dublin	
		Ringerike art style in Ireland
1100		Production of 'Brian's Saga' Urnes art style in Ireland
		Vikings feature in Irish folk tradition

BIBLIOGRAPHY

Primary Sources

For descriptions of early Scandinavia see:
Adam of Bremen, *History of the Archbishops of Hamburg-Bremen*. trans. F.J. Tschan. New York, 1975.
Ohthere's account, in N. Lund et al. (eds.), *Two Voyagers at the Court of King Alfred*. York, 1984.

For accounts of the Viking attacks on Continental Europe, Britain and Ireland see:
Adam of Bremen, *History of the Archbishops of Hamburg-Bremen*. trans. F.J. Tschan. New York, 1975.
Carolingian Chronicles. ed. B.W. Scholtz. Ann Arbor, Michigan, 1970.
The Anglo-Saxon Chronicle. ed. Benjamin Thorpe. London, 1861.
The Annals of Ulster (to A.D. 1131). ed. Seán MacAirt & Gearóid MacNiocaill. Dublin, 1983.
The Fragmentary Annals of Ireland. ed. Joan N. Radner. Dublin, 1978.
D. Whitelock (ed. and trans.), *English Historical Documents c. 500–1042*. 2 vols. 2nd ed. London, 1979.
A.O. Anderson (ed. and trans.), *Early Sources of Scottish History A.D. 500–1286*. Edinburgh, 1922.

For Irish Literary Perspectives on the 'Viking Age' see:
Cogadh Gáedhel re Gallaibh. ed. James Henthorn Todd. London, 1867.
Thesaurus Paleohibernicus: a collection of Old Irish glosses, scholia, prose and verse. ed. Whitley Stokes & John Strachan. 2 vols Cambridge, 1901–03.
The Metrical Dindshenchas. 5 parts. ed. Edmund J. Gwynn. Dublin, 1903.

For accounts of Irish voyages see:
Adomnán of Iona, *Life of St. Columba*. trans. Richard Sharpe. London, 1995.
Dícuil, *The Book of the measurement of the Earth*. ed. J.J. Tierney. Dublin, 1967.
The Voyage of St. Brendan. trans. J.J. O'Meara. Portlaoise, 1981.

For Scandinavian Literary Perspectives on the 'post Viking Age' see
Njal's Saga. ed. Magnus Magnusson & Hermann Pálsson. London, 1960.
The North Atlantic Saga. ed. Gwyn Jones. Oxford & New York, 1964.

Secondary Sources

Arbman, Erik Holger. *The Vikings*. London, 1961; Boulder, Colorado, 1961.
Ashe, Geoffrey et al. *The Quest for America*. London, 1971.
Binchy, D.A. 'The passing of the Old Order'. pp. 119–32. in Ó Cuív, Brian (ed.), *The Impact of the Scandinavian Invasions on the Celtic-speaking peoples. c. 800–1100 A.D.* Dublin, 1962.

Bradley, John (ed.). *Settlement and Society in Medieval Ireland.* Kilkenny, 1988.

Bradley, John. 'Scandinavian Settlement', in Bradley, J. (ed.), *Settlement and Society.* Kilkenny, 1988.

Bradley, John & Halpin, Andrew. 'Topographical Development of Scandinavian and Anglo-Norman Waterford', pp. 15–44, in W. Nolan & T.P. Power (eds.), *Waterford: History and Society.* Dublin, 1992.

Bradley, John & Halpin, Andrew. 'Topographical Development of Scandinavian and Anglo-Norman Cork', pp. 15–44, in P. O'Flanagan & C.G. Buttimer (eds.), *Cork: History and Society.* Dublin, 1993.

Brent, Peter. *The Viking Saga.* London, 1975.

Byrne, Francis John. *Irish Kings and High Kings.* London, 1973; new ed. Dublin, 2001.

Charles-Edwards, Thomas. 'Irish Warfare before 1100'. pp. 26–51, in T. Bartlett & K. Jeffrey (eds.), *A Military History of Ireland.* Cambridge, 1996.

Clarke, H.B., Ní Mhaonaigh, M. & Ó Floinn, R. (eds.). *Ireland and Scandinavia in the Early Viking Age.* Dublin, 1998.

Clarke, H B. 'Proto-towns and Towns in Ireland and Britain in the Ninth and Tenth Centuries'. pp. 331–80, in Clarke, H.B. et al. (eds.), *Ireland and Scandinavia in the Early Viking Age.* Dublin, 1998.

Clarke, Howard B. 'Conversion, Church and cathedral: the diocese of Dublin to 1152'. pp. 19–50, in J. Kelly & D. Keogh (eds.), *History of the Catholic Diocese of Dublin.* Dublin, 2000.

Doherty, Charles. 'The Vikings in Ireland: a Review'. pp. 288–330, in Clarke, H.B. et al. (eds.), *Ireland and Scandinavia in the Early Viking Age.* Dublin, 1998.

Duffy, S. 'Irishmen and Islesmen in the kingdoms of Dublin and Man, 1052–1171', *Ériu,* xliii (1992), 93–133.

Edwards, Nancy. *The Archaeology of Early Medieval Ireland.* London, 1990. (Chapter 8)

Etchingham, Colmán. *Viking Raids on Irish Church Settlements in the ninth century.* Maynooth, 1996.

Etchingham, Colmán. 'Evidence of Scandinavian Settlement in Co. Wicklow', pp. 113–38. in K. Hannigan & W. Nolan (eds.), *Wicklow: History and Society.* Dublin, 1994.

Fenton, Alexander & Pálsson, Hermann (eds.). *The Northern and Western Isles in the Viking World: Survival, Continuity and Change.* Edinburgh, 1984.

Foote, P. & Wilson, D. *The Viking Achievement.* London, 1970; New York, 1970.

Graham-Campbell, James. *The Viking World.* revised ed. London, 1989.

Graham-Campbell, James. 'From Scandinavia to the Irish Sea: Viking Art Reviewed'. in Michael Ryan (ed.), *Ireland and Insular Art.* Dublin, 1987.

Helle, Knut. 'The History of the Early Viking Age in Norway'. pp. 239–58, in Clarke, H.B. et al. (eds.), *Ireland and Scandinavia in the Early Viking Age.* Dublin, 1998.

Henry, Francoise. *Irish Art during the Viking Invasions (800–1020 A.D.).* London, 1967.

Henry, Francoise. *Irish Art in the Romanesque Period (1020–1170 A.D.).* London, 1970.

Herbert, Máire. *Iona, Kells and Derry.* Oxford, 1988. (chapter 5)

Hurley, Maurice F. 'Below Sea-level in the City of Cork', pp. 41–54, in H.B. Clarke (ed.), *Irish Cities.* Cork & Dublin, 1995.

Jesch, Judith. *Women in the Viking Age.* Woodbridge, 1991.

Jones, Gwyn. *A History of the Vikings.* New York, 1968.

Kelleher, John V. 'The Rise of the Dál Cais'. pp. 230–41, in E. Rynne (ed.), *Nth Munster Studies: Essays in Commemoration of Mgr. M. Moloney.* Limerick, 1967.

Kristjánsson, Jónas. 'Ireland and the Irish in Icelandic Tradition'. pp. 259–76, in Clarke, H.B. et al. (eds.), *Ireland and Scandinavia in the Early Viking Age.* Dublin, 1998.

Logan, F. D. *The Vikings in History.* London, 1983.

Lucas, A. T. 'Irish-Norse relations: time for reappraisal?'. *Jnl. Cork Hist. and Arch. Soc.*, 71 (1966), 62–75.

Lucas, A. T. 'The plundering and burning of churches in Ireland, 7th to 16th centuries', pp. 172–229. in E. Rynne (ed.), *Nth Munster Studies: Essays in Commemoration of Mgr. M. Moloney.* Limerick, 1967.

MacShamhráin, Ailbhe. *Church and Polity in pre-Norman Ireland.* Maynooth, 1996.

MacShamhráin, Ailbhe. 'The battle of Glenn Máma, Dublin and the High-Kingship of Ireland'. pp. 53–64, in Seán Duffy (ed.), *Medieval Dublin II.* Dublin, 2001.

Marcus, G.J. *The Conquest of the North Atlantic.* Woodbridge, 1980.

Meldgaard, Jørgen et al. *Viking Voyages to North America.* Roskilde, 1993.

Morris, Christopher. 'Raiders, Traders and Settlers: the Early Viking Age in Scotland'. pp. 73–103, in Clarke, H.B. et al. (eds.), *Ireland and Scandinavia in the Early Viking Age.* Dublin, 1998.

Myhre, Bjørn. 'The Archaeology of the Early Viking Age in Norway'. pp. 3–36, in Clarke, H.B. et al. (eds.), *Ireland and Scandinavia in the Early Viking Age.* Dublin, 1998.

Ní Mhaonaigh, Máire. 'Friend and Foe: Vikings in Ninth and Tenth Century Irish Literature'. pp. 381–404, in Clarke, H.B. et al (eds.), *Ireland and Scandinavia in the Early Viking Age.* Dublin, 1998.

Ó Corráin, Donnchadh. 'Viking Ireland: Afterthoughts'. pp. 421–52, in Clarke, H.B. et al. (eds.), *Ireland and Scandinavia in the Early Viking Age.* Dublin, 1998.

Ó Corráin, Donncha. *Ireland before the Normans.* Dublin, 1972.

Ó Cróinín, Dáibhí. *Early Medieval Ireland.* London, 1995.

Ó Cuív, Brian. 'Personal Names', in Bradley, J. (ed.), *Settlement and Society.* Kilkenny, 1988.

Ó Cuív, Brian (ed.), *Impact of the Scandinavian Invasions on the Celtic-speaking peoples. c. 800–1100 A.D.* Proceedings of the first International Congress of Celtic Studies. Dublin, 1962.

Ó Floinn, Raghnall. 'The Archaeology of the Early Viking Age in Ireland'. pp. 131–165, in Clarke, H.B. et al. (eds.), *Ireland and Scandinavia in the Early Viking Age.* Dublin, 1998.

O'Rahilly, C. 'Medieval Limerick', in H.B. Clarke (ed.), *Irish Cities.* Cork & Dublin, 1995.

Oxenstierna, Erik. *The World of the Norsemen.* transl. Janet Sondheimer. London, 1975.

Page, R. I. *Chronicles of the Vikings.* London, 1995.

Page, R .I. *Norse Myths.* London, 1990.

Pedersen, Ole Crumlin. *Aspects of Maritime Scandinavia.* Roskilde, 1991.

Rekdal, Jan Erik. 'Parallels between the Norwegian Legend of St. Sunniva and Irish Voyage Tales'. pp. 277–87, in Clarke, H.B. et al. (eds.), *Ireland and Scandinavia in the Early Viking Age.* Dublin, 1998.

Roesdahl, Else. *The Vikings.* London, 1991.

Roesdahl, Else et al. (eds.), *The Vikings in England.* London, 1981.

Ryan, John. 'Brian Bóruma, king of Ireland'. pp. 355–74, in E. Rynne (ed.), *Nth Munster Studies: Essays in Commemoration of Mgr. M. Moloney.* Limerick, 1967.

Sawyer, B. & Sawyer, P. *Medieval Scandinavia: from Conversion to Reformation, A.D. 800–1500.* Minneapolis and London, 1993.

Sawyer, P.H. *The Age of the Vikings.* rev. ed. London, 1971.

Sawyer, Peter. 'The Vikings and Ireland'. pp. 345–61, in D. Whitelock et. al. (eds.), *Ireland in Early Medieval Europe.* Cambridge, 1982.

Sawyer, Peter. *Kings and Vikings: Scandinavia and Europe A.D. 700–1100.* London & New York, 1982.

Simpson, Jacqueline. *The Viking World.* London, 1980.

Simpson, Linzi. 'Forty years a' digging: a preliminary synthesis of archaeological investigations in medieval Dublin'. pp. 11–68, in Seán Duffy (ed.), *Medieval Dublin I.* Dublin, 2000.

Smyth, Alfred P. *Scandinavian York and Dublin.* 2 vols. Dublin, 1975; 1979.

Smyth, Alfred P. *Scandinavian Kings in the British Isles, 850–880.* Oxford, 1977.

Smyth, Alfred P. *Warlords and Holy Men: Scotland A.D. 80–1000.* Edinburgh, 1984. (Chapter 5)

Valante, Mary. 'Dublin's Economic relations with Hinterland and Periphery in the Later Viking Age'. pp. 69–83, in Seán Duffy (ed.), *Medieval Dublin I.* Dublin, 2000.

Wallace, Patrick. 'The emergence of Dublin', in Bradley, J. (ed.), *Settlement and Society.* Kilkenny, 1988.

Wallace, Patrick F. 'The Archaeological Identity of the Hiberno-Norse Town', *Jnl. Roy. Soc. Antiq. Ire.*, 122 (1992), 35–66.

Wallace, Patrick F. '*Garrda* and *airbeada*: the plot thickens in Viking Dublin', pp. 261–74, in A.P. Smyth (ed.), *Seanchas: Studies in Early and Medieval Irish Archaeology, History and Literature in honour of Francis J. Byrne.* Dublin, 2000.

Wilson, David. *The Vikings and their Origins.* London, 1970.

Wooding, Jonathan. *Communication and Commerce along the Western Sealanes, A.D. 400–800.* (BAR International Series, 654). Oxford, 1996.

Wooding, Jonathan. 'St. Brendan's Boat: Dead Hides and the Living Sea'. pp. 77–92, in J. Carey, M. Herbert & P. Ó Riain (eds.), *Studies in Irish Hagiography: Saints and Scholars.* Dublin, 2001.

CREDITS

Acknowledgements

Grateful thanks to the following publishers for kindly permitting reproduction of copyright material in the form of extracts from documentary sources:

Dublin Institute for Advanced Studies; extracts from J.J. Tierney (ed.), Dícuil: *Book of the Measurement of the Earth* (Dublin, 1967).

Oxford University Press; extracts from Gwyn Jones (trans.), *The Norse Atlantic Saga: being the Norse Voyages of Discovery and Settlement to Iceland, Greenland and North America*. 2nd edition (Oxford, 1986).

Penguin Books Ltd.; extracts from Richard Sharpe (trans.), *Life of St. Columba* by Adomnán of Iona (London, 1995); Magnus Magnusson & Herman Pálsson (trans.), *Njal's Saga* (London, 1960); J.J. O'Meara (trans.), *The History and Topography of Ireland* by Gerald of Wales (London, 1982).

Professor emeritus J.J. O'Meara; extracts from his translation of *The Voyage of St. Brendan* (Port Laoise: Dolmen Press, 1981).

Sessions of York/Ebor Press; extracts from N. Lund et al. (eds.), Two Voyagers at the Court of King Alfred (York, 1984).

Picture acknowledgements

Black and white picture credits
Courtesy AKG London pp frontispiece (Statens Historiska Museum, Stockholm), 10, 15, 16, 19, 22, 27, 39, 40, 41, 44, 81 (Photo: Jürgen Sorges), 89, 103 (Photo: Erick Lessing);
D'Alton's *History of Ireland* p 64;
Danish Tourist Board p 79;
Kind courtesy of Margaret Gowen & Co. Ltd., pp 95 (left), photographs by Mark Morahan, 91 (top), 93 (right and bottom), 95 (top and bottom), 99, 100, 101 (left), photographs by Brendan Dempsey, 91 (right), 93 (top), 101 (top), 113, 114, 116;
National Museum of Ireland pp 34, 35, 36, 37, 38, 54, 57, 97, 110 (top and bottom), 111, 112, 115, 117;
© National Geographic Society 1970, paintings by Tom Lovell, pp 73, 83, 103;
Private collections pp 21 modern drawing from *The Saga of Olaf Tryggvason*, 103 Modern drawing from *The Saga of Olaf Tryggvason* (London, 1911), 118 drawing by Patrick O'Byrne, 1919;

Colour Plates:
Photo: Bergen Reiselivslag p 1 (top); Royal Danish Ministry of Foreign Affairs p 1 (bottom);
Willy Haraldsen/Norwegian Tourist Board p 2 (top); National Museum of Ireland p 2 (bottom);
Courtesy AKG London/British Library p 3;
Kind courtesy of Margaret Gowen & Co. Ltd., photographs by Mark Morahan, p 4;
National Museum of Ireland p 5 (top); Margaret Gowen & Co. Ltd., photo: Brendan Demspey p 5 (bottom);
AKG London p 6 (top); Painting by Christian Krohg, Norway. Courtesy Nasjonalgalleriet, Oslo p 6 (bottom);
Photo: Jürgen Sorges. Courtesy AKG London p 7 (top); Photo: Erich Lessing. Courtesy AKG London p 7 (bottom);
British Museum: AKG London p 8.

INDEX

Adam of Bremen, 11, 12, 17, 25, 26, 28, 104
Adomnán of Iona, 70–1
Áed Finnliath, King of Ailech, 49, 51
Aethelred, King of Northumbria, 34
agriculture, 14, 16–18, 88–90
Alcuin of York, 9, 34–5
Alfred the Great, King, 11–12, 13
Altuna stone, Uppland, 27
amber, 94, 98
America, 10, 13, 80–5, 105–6
Amlaíb Cuarán, King of Dublin, 58–9, 60–1, 62, 65, 117
Anglo-Saxon Chronicle, 49
Annagassan, Co. Louth, 43, 44
Annals of Ulster, 37, 51, 57, 63
Anund Jakob, King, 104
Ari Frodi, 72–3, 75
Armagh, 42, 57, 58, 64, 117
Athelstan, King, 58, 102
Athlunkard, Co. Limerick, 44
Audr, wife of Olafr, 76, 104

Baffin Island, 83, 85
Ballinderry game board, 111
Ballyholme, Co. Down, 54
Ballywillin, Co. Antrim, 54
Barith, magnate, 50–1, 53
Beginish, Co. Kerry, 56
Birka, 20, 115
blacksmithing, 92
Blathmac of Iona, 39, 40
'blood-eagling,' 40
bone working, 21, 31, 95, 96, 100, 116
Borgund church, 103
Borre, 17, 26
Bostrand hoard, 98
Brendan the Navigator, St, 71–2, 80, 84, 102
Brian Boruma, High King of Ireland, 61-2, 63–5, 67, 111
'Brian's Saga,' 77, 78, 119
Bride Street, Dublin, 102
Britain, 13, 34, 48, 56, 67, 68, 87
  first viking attack, 31
  placenames, 88–9
  trade, 98
  viking settlements, 43, 49, 53, 55, 58
Brunanburh, battle of, 58

Cainnech (Mo-Chainne), St, 102
Castledermot, Co. Kildare, 58
Cathach, Shrine of the, 116–17
cemeteries, 26, 45
Cenn Fuait, battle of, 54–5
Cerball, son of Dúngal, King of Osraige, 50, 78
Cherrywood, Co. Dublin, 45, 90
Chester, 98
Christ Church cathedral, Dublin, 100
Christchurch Place, Dublin, 92
Christianity, 28–9, 31, 73, 74, 81
  in Ireland, 33
  role of, 99–100, 102–6
Clonmacnois, 36, 58
Clontarf, battle of, 65–8, 78, 87
clothing, 23–4
Cluain Crema, Co. Roscommon, 36
Cnut, king, 67
Cogadh Gaedhel re Gallaib, 43, 46, 47, 61, 63, 87, 96
  battle of Clontarf, 66, 67
coinage, 21, 60, 62–3, 96–7, 113
Columba, St, 59–60, 100, 104, 117
Confey, Co. Dublin, 54–5
Congalach, son of Máel-mithig, King of Tara, 57, 58
crafts, 20–1, 92–6
Cuerdale Hoard, 53

Dal Cais, 47, 61–8
decorative styles, 30, 116–17
Denmark, 11, 12, 20, 28, 67, 94
  agriculture, 14
  centralised, 29
  Christianity, 28, 102
  settlements, 22
  ship burials, 26
  towns, 115
  trade, 31
  vikings from, 47–8, 49, 53
Diarmait, son of Máele-na-mbó, King of Uí Cheinnselaig, 68, 78
Dicuil of Iona, 11, 72, 74
Donemuthan monastery, 34
Donnchad, son of Briain Bóruma, 68
Donnchad, grandson of Máel-Sechnaill, King of Tara, 58
dress, 23–4
Dubgennti, 47–8

Dublin, kingdom of, 45, 74, 81, 100, 102, 115, 119
  agriculture, 89
  burials, 38, 45
  crafts, 92–6
  early foundation, 49–51
  excavations, 57, 90, 91, 92, 94
  Hiberno-Scandinavian kings, 59
  and Icelandic settlement, 76–7
  Irish control of, 62–8
  original site of, 45–6
  power-politics, 56–61
  Scandinavian kings, 48
  trade, 96–9
Duiblinn, 43, 45–6

Echmarcach, King, 68
Eddaic verse, 25, 28
Eiriks saga rauda, 82
Erik Gnupsson, Bishop, 105–6
Erik the Red, 81–2, 105
Eriks saga rauda, 84
Esjuberg church, 104
Essex Street, Dublin, 45
Estonia, 14
Etar, Co. Dublin, 42
Etgal of Scellig, 42

Faroe Islands, 17, 28, 31, 38, 71, 72, 76, 79
  Christianity, 105
  hermits, 73–4
Fedelmid mac Crimthainn, King, 36
Fianna, the, 118, 119
Findan of Rheinau, 42
Finland, 12
Fishamble Street, Dublin, 94, 97
fishing, 90, 92, 112
Forrach, Co. Meath, 47
Fragmentary Annals of Ireland, 50, 78
France, 34, 43, 87, 98
Francia, 49, 51
Frey, 27
Freya, 27–8
Frostuping, 24

game board, 111
Gerald of Wales, 109
Germany, 102
Glenn Máma, battle of, 63
Glúniarann, King of Dublin, 62

Godred, King of Denmark, 34
Gokstad, 20, 48
Gormlaith, wife of Amlaíb
    Cuarán, 59, 65
Gothfrith, King of Dublin, 48,
    53, 55, 58
Gotland, 12, 20, 23
Graenlendinga saga, 82, 85
Greenland, 81–5, 88, 89, 99,
    105–6
Grim Kamban, 76
Grimestad hoard, 98
Gunnbjorn Ulf Krakason,
    navigator, 81

Hafrsfjord, battle of, 75
Hakon, King of Norway, 102
Halfdan, King, 50–1, 53
Halogaland, 11–12, 17–18
Harald Bluetooth, King of
    Denmark, 102
Haraldr, King of Limerick,
    55–6, 61, 62
Haraldr harfagri, King of
    Norway, 29, 75–6
health, 23
Hebrides 37, 48, 65, 68, 70, 76,
    78, see also Western Isles
Hedeby, 20, 21, 29, 115
Heimskringla, 40
Hel, 28
hermits, 70–5
High Street, Dublin, 57, 96
Hordaland, 31
housing, 22–4

Ibn Fadhlan, 25, 26
Iceland, 17, 28, 71, 73
    Christianity, 29, 104–5
    sagas, 118–19
    settlement of, 75–9
Ile de Noirmoutier, 43
Ingólfr, 76, 77
inheritance, laws of, 25
Inis Patraic, 37–8
Inishboffin, 37
Inishmurray, 37, 38
Inuit people, 79, 80, 81, 84
Inuk people, 85, 106
Iona, 37, 38, 40, 60, 72, 100
Ireland, 13, 31, 33, 87
houses, 23
influence of vikings, 108–19
'invasion' and resistance, 42–7
    Scandinavian kingdoms,
    53–6, 61–8
    sources of viking raids, 36–9

viking raids, 35–6, 39–42
viking settlements, 47–51
vikings and Irish politics,
    56–61, 108–9
Irish language, 112–14
Iron Age, 12, 14, 22, 26–7, 30
ironworking, 18, 20, 92
Islandbridge, Dublin, 38, 45, 55
Isle of Man, 53, 54, 58, 63, 65,
    68, 78, 88, 90
Islendingabok, 72–3, 75, 81
Ívarr, King of Dublin
    Norsemen, 48–51, 53
Ívarr, King of Limerick, 62

Jelling, 14, 102
picture-stone, 15
jewellery, 20, 30, 35, 92, 94, 95,
    98, 99, 113, 114
Julius Solinus, 11
Jutland, 12, 14, 22, 28, 29, 102

Kaupang, 60, 115
Kells, 40, 58, 72, 117
Ketill Flatnef, magnate, 49
Ketill inn fiflski, 76, 104
Kevin Street, Dublin, 102
Kilcullen, 58
Kildare, 58
Kilmainham burials, 45

Lambay Island, 37
Landnamabók, 73, 75, 76, 77–8,
    79, 80
languages, 12–13, 112–14
L'Anse aux Meadows, 85, 99
Latvia, 14
laws, 24–5
leatherworking, 21, 36, 96
Leif Eriksson, 81–2, 83
Leif (Hjor Leif), 76, 77
Leixlip, Co. Dublin, 56, 90
Liffey River, 43, 46, 55, 90, 96
Limerick, 55–6, 61, 63, 96, 115
Lindisfarne, 9, 34
Linn Duachaill, Co. Louth,
    43
literature, 117–19
Loch Dá Caech, Co. Waterford,
    53
Lofoten, 22
longphoirt, 43–5

MacLochlainn, Domnall, King
    of Cenél nEogain, 117
Máelmorda, King of Uí
    Dúnlainge, 65, 66

Máel-Sechnaill, son of
    Domnall, King of Tara, 47,
    60, 62, 63, 64, 78
Magnus, King of Norway, 78
Magnus the Great, 118
Mathgamain, son of Cennétig,
    King of Cashel, 61
metal working, 92, 101
Michan, St, 102
monasticism, 108
Moore, Thomas, 62
Murchad, King of Dublin, 68
Murchad, King of Uí
    Dúnlainge, 59

names, personal, 77, 114
Newfoundland, 85, 99, 106
Niall Glúndub, King of Tara, 55
Njal's Saga, 65, 105
Normandy, 13, 74, 87, 88, 99, 100
Norrland, 18
Northern Isles, 17, 37–9, 48, 56,
    58, 63, 68, 98
    hermits, 70–1
Northumbria, 34, 50–1, 53, 55
Norway, 11–12, 13, 14, 18, 25, 117
    agriculture, 14, 16–18
    centralisation, 29, 30, 67
    Christianity, 28, 100, 102–6
    coinage, 21
    hoards, 98
    Icelandic settlement, 75–6,
    104–5
    settlements, 22, 23
    ship burials, 26
    towns, 115
    vikings from, 38–9, 48, 49,
    53, 55, 99

Odin, 27, 28
Offa, King, 34
ogham, 71
Ólafr (Amlaíb), King of Dublin
    Norsemen, 48–51, 76
Ólafr (Amlaíb Cuarán), King of
    Dublin. See Amlaíb Cuarán
Ólafr Gothfrithsson, King of
    Dublin, 55, 56, 58
Ólafr Haraldsson, King of
    Norway, 28, 100, 102–3
Ólafr the magnate see Ólafr
    Kings of Dublin Norsemen
Ólafr Skotkonung, King of
    Svear and Gotar, 29, 104
Ólafr Tryggvason, King of
    Norway, 28, 83, 102, 103, 105
Olave, St. see Ólafr Haraldsson

O'Riordan, Brendan, 57
Orkney, 31, 37, 38, 39, 65-6, 90, *see also* Northern Isles
hermits, 70
Oseberg, 14, 16, 20, 39
Ottarr of Halogaland, 11-12, 13, 17-18
Oxmantown, Dublin, 102

papar, 71-4
Patrick, St, 100
Patrick Street, Dublin, 102
Picts, 38, 70
picture-stones, 15, 22, 23
placenames, 30, 56, 71, 77, 88-9, 90
Plinius Secundus (Pliny), 11
Poddle River, 45
poetry, 25, 39, 117
Provincial Laws, 25

Quentovic, 43

Ragnall (Rognvald), magnate, 53-4, 54, 55
Ragnar Lodbrók, King, 48
Rathlin, Co. Antrim, 37
Ravensdale, Co. Dublin, 56
Rechru, raid on, 37
religion, 25-9
Ringerike style, 116-17
Rogaland, 26, 29, 75
Roskilde ship, 94, 98
rune-stones, 14, 19, 25, 117
runic alphabet, 12
Russia, 13, 87, 103, 104

Saami, the, 12, 18
sagas, 118-19
St Cuthbert, church of, 34-5
St Michael le Pole, church of, 45
St Patrick's bell, shrine of, 117
St Philibert, monastery of, 34
Saxolb, chieftain, 42
Scattery Island, 62
Scellig Mhichíl, Co. Kerry, 42
Scotland, 48, 55, 56, 70, 98
agriculture, 90
viking raids, 37

Selja, holy men of, 102
settlements, 22-4
urban, 114-16
Shetland, 23, 31, 37, 38, 39, 70-1, 90, *see also* Northern Isles
ship burials, 26, 27, 54
shipbuilding, 20, 94, 112
Sigmund Brestisson, 105
Sitriuc, magnate, 53, 54-5, 55, 58
Sitriuc, son of Ivarr, 51
Sitriuc Silkenbeard, King of Dublin, 59, 61, 62, 63, 65, 97
founds Christ Church, 100
'Skraelings,' 80, 84, 85
slavery, 21, 24, 41-2, 98
Smaland, 18
Smerwick, 90
Sord Coluim Cille, Co. Dublin, 59-60
Stengade burial, 26
stone working, 20, 94, 98, 101
Sulchóit, battle of, 61
Sunniva, St, 102
Sweden, 11, 12, 14, 18, 20, 27, 28
agriculture, 14
centralisation, 29, 30
Christianity, 104
coinage, 21
towns, 115

Tara, battle of, 62
Temnen, anchorite, 40
Temple Bar, Dublin, 45, 91, 101
textiles, 21, 24, 96
Thor, 27, 28
Thorfinn Karlsefni, 83, 85
Thorstein Eriksson, 83
Thorvald Eriksson, 83, 84
trade, 21, 30-1, 60, 96-9
settlements, 44-5
transport, 14
Trondelag, 18, 28, 67
Turgesius, King, 46, 47
Ua Briain dynasty, 68, 78, 111-12
Ua Domnaill, Cathbarr, King of Cenél Lugdach, 117

ua hArtacáin, Cinaed, 59, 60
Uí Cheinnselaig, the, 68
Uí Dúnlainge, the, 33, 46, 58, 59, 63, 65, 68
Uí Néill, the, 33, 46, 47, 49, 57-8, 62-3, 64, 68
Umall, King of, 36
urban settlement, 114-16
Urnes style, 117

Valhalla, 26-7
Vestfold, 29, 38, 48
Vestmannaeyjar Islands, 77
vikings, 11
agricultural economy, 14, 16-18
definition of, 9
health, 23
houses, 22-4
industry and crafts, 18, 20-1
Irish settlements, 47-51
languages of, 12-13
long-term influence of, 108-19
movement abroad, 29-31
religion, 25-9
seen as pirates, 33-6
social organisation, 24-5
sources of, 36-9
Vinland, 80-1, 83-4, 88

Walafrid Strabo, 39
warfare, 87-8, 109-12
Waterford, 53, 54, 55, 62, 63, 92, 102, 115
weapons, 37, 87, 98, 110, 111
weights, 21, 96, 113
Western Isles, 62, 78, 81, 119
Wexford, 89, 90, 92, 96
Whitefriar Street, Dublin, 45
Winetavern Street, Dublin, 94
Wood Quay, Dublin, 90
wood working, 20-1, 54, 93, 94, 95

York, 55, 58, 98, 100, 115
Yorkshire, 88, 89